THE QUEST FOR CHRISTIAN UNITY

HADDAM HOUSE is a publishing project in the field of religious literature for youth. Its special concern is the moral and religious questions and needs of young men and women. It gathers up and continues the interests that led to the publication of the Hazen Books on Religion and is directed primarily to students and employed young people.

Haddam House seeks as authors new voices qualified to give fresh guidance to thoughtful youth. In consultation with leaders of the United Student Christian Council and other groups, Haddam House is studying the changing needs for literature in its field and developing methods of wide distribution.

Haddam House Books to Date

BEYOND THIS DARKNESS, *Roger L. Shinn*

CHRISTIAN FAITH AND MY JOB, *Alexander Miller*

PRIMER FOR PROTESTANTS, *James Hastings Nichols*

PREFACE TO ETHICAL LIVING, *Robert E. Fitch*

THE GRAND INQUISITOR, *Fyodor Dostoevsky*

CHRISTIANITY AND COMMUNISM, *John C. Bennett*

YOUTH ASKS ABOUT RELIGION, *Jack Finegan*

YOUNG LAYMEN—YOUNG CHURCH, *John Oliver Nelson*

THE HUMAN VENTURE IN SEX, LOVE, AND MARRIAGE, *Peter A. Bertocci*

SCIENCE AND CHRISTIAN FAITH, *Edward LeRoy Long, Jr.*

A GOSPEL FOR THE SOCIAL AWAKENING, *Rauschenbusch*

THE CHRISTIAN IN POLITICS, *Jerry Voorhis*

REDISCOVERING THE BIBLE, *Bernhard W. Anderson*

LIFE'S MEANING, *Henry P. Van Dusen*

THAT ALL MAY BE ONE, *James Edward Lesslie Newbigin*

THE CHRISTIAN STUDENT AND THE CHURCH, *J. Robert Nelson, Editor*

THE CHRISTIAN STUDENT AND THE UNIVERSITY, *J. Robert Nelson, Editor*

THE CHRISTIAN STUDENT AND THE WORLD STRUGGLE, *J. Robert Nelson, Editor*

THE QUEST FOR CHRISTIAN UNITY, *Robert S. Bilheimer*

THE QUEST

for

CHRISTIAN

UNITY

BY

Robert S. Bilheimer

A Haddam   *House Book*

ASSOCIATION PRESS

NEW YORK

1

The Haddam House Editorial Board wishes to express its appreciation to the persons who have prepared the denominational statements which constitute Part Two of this book. Their contribution to the whole is of the utmost importance.

The Board also wishes to acknowledge its debt to the book, In Search of Unity, *brief outline studies comparing the teachings of the British churches, and edited by Denis E. Taylor. This was the book that suggested to the Board the present volume, which Mr. Bilheimer was asked to write.*

October, 1952

Contents

PART ONE

Introduction

THE PURPOSE OF this book is to give an account of the quest
for unity among Christians and the churches during the past
half century. This quest, beginning modestly, has now reached
the proportions of a world movement and is embodied in many
different structures and forms. Because of its comparatively recent rise, because of its complexity, because of the dangers it
faces and the promise it holds, this quest should always be
held within a certain perspective.

Actually three different perspectives are necessary, of which
the first is historical. In the early centuries of the church,
denominations as we know them did not exist. There was, on
the whole, a fairly recognizable common body of conviction,
practice, and life within the Christian church, which found its
expression in different localities in the Mediterranean world.
There were divisions, but these were divisions which were
largely heresies or near heresies. There were, as we know from
the Bible, those who, in the very early days, wanted to make
Christianity another edition of Judaism, as well as those who
followed Paul and Peter and Apollos. In later times there were
the Montanists, the Gnostics, the Donatists, the Arians, the
Nestorians, to mention the more prominent, together with
other variations of interpretations. Ruled by the chief body of
the church as either heretical or schismatic, nearly all of them
ultimately died out. From one viewpoint, they are testimony
to the fact that the church has always been torn by divisions.
From another viewpoint, it can be maintained that a central

unity of conviction and practice was maintained. The beginnings of great and permanent schism, however, soon began to
be felt. Two empires, and with them two centers of Christian
life, Rome and Constantinople, were in deadly rivalry. Different interests in the Christian faith began to be noticeable.
Tension developing into conflict and conflict developing into
open division led ultimately to the Great Schism between East
and West, the East being that which we now know as the Orthodox, and the West being Catholic with its center at Rome. By
the twelfth century this western Roman Catholicism was at its
height, that truly glorious height in which the integration of
society with Christianity was so dramatically achieved, of which
the cathedrals are the magnificent expressions, of which the
great civilizing work of the monasteries was also a part. The
church was divided, the Christians of the East and the Christians of the West not being in communion with each other,
Christians of the East bitter against the violent inroads of the
Crusaders from the West. Yet there was unity within each of
the two great divisions. In the West, however, that unity was
even at its height beginning to crack. Theological thought,
philosophical inquiry, biblical conviction, and mystical experience joined with certain as yet hardly recognized influences
of society to provide a restlessness within the structure of
unity. This restlessness became more pronounced. By the sixteenth century it exploded, and the unity of western Christendom was shattered.

From this point on the account is one, first, of extreme
multiplication of sects. As we shall see, in Europe and Britain
and in the United States, self-contained churches arose around
great and small points of doctrine alike. These were reinforced
by national interests and to some extent by economic ones as
well. Only in comparatively recent times, on the whole during

the past half century, has the process of almost endless division become reversed. These now autonomous churches have begun to seek each other out, and in so doing have begun to form a new kind of unity—different from that of the early church, different from that of the medieval church.

Two factors in this modern development must be specially mentioned here. The first is that for the first time the churches of the East are being brought into contact with churches of the West. The depth of the ancient schism still remains, as anyone in the ecumenical movement—whether from the East or from the West—will readily testify. But the sting is gone, and contact is possible. From the viewpoint of the Orthodox, it is contact with something new. It is not contact with the church with which there was the original schism. It is contact with churches which on the whole and in the majority are the products of the Reformation, an experience of church history which the Orthodox did not undergo and from which they were always remote. In this fact itself lies a complication of great magnitude for present ecumenical discussion.

The second factor is that the Roman Catholic Church is not a party to the present ecumenical movement. She is not by her own choice and by virtue of her own position. From her viewpoint, she is the only true church on earth, Christ having passed his authority and his work exclusively to her. Union with Rome is possible, and can be discussed, only on the basis of a return to her basic position. She cannot and will not talk with churches which demand that they be recognized as churches. She can only talk as the true and righteous talk with the schismatic and heretic, with a view to their correction. For this reason the Roman Church does not appear in ecumenical discussion. Because of this fact, we shall not deal with the

Roman Catholic Church and shall use the terms "church" and "churches" as excluding Rome.

A second perspective is the perspective of the street corner. It is of basic and urgent importance that everyone concerned with Christian unity keep this perspective constantly in mind. It is the perspective that feels the demands of the world, the world which hungers for faith and for a demonstration of Christian righteousness, and which is largely fed with a hesitant babble. It is the perspective which sees, on nearly any street corner, numerous churches without demonstrable relationship to each other, living in much isolation from each other, in competition much of the time with each other. The danger of this perspective, if we never lift our eyes from the street corner, is that we become completely discouraged. It all takes such a long time! And in becoming discouraged we are tempted to advocate that kind of superficial and quick unity among the churches which will have no lasting basis. The greater value of this perspective is the obvious one: it adds the right kind of urgency to our quest for unity, which was once supplied by our Lord himself—"that the world may *believe*."

A third perspective is that of the ecumenical movement itself. It is a perspective which on the one hand shows a very decided, almost miraculous advance, and on the other hand reveals to sober judgment a host of very serious and real problems. That there is progress cannot be denied. Even in the early days of our country Christians were for the most part not even on speaking terms with each other across their denominational barriers, unless it was to hurl an almost unbelievably violent invective at their fellow members of the Body of Christ. With only one or two notable exceptions, they did not cooperate with each other that the world might believe, and hardly did they dream of it. Today, as it is our purpose to relate, this is a radically changed picture. Yet great problems remain, as it is also our purpose to indicate. The danger of the perspective of the ecumenical movement is that we become romantic about it, glorying in our achievements but failing to see with our hearts as well as our minds the immense problems yet to be faced and the great distance still to be traveled. We are also in danger of a preoccupation with the mechanics of our ecumenical life, tempted to feel that a structure of inter-denominational committees, a program of interdenominational conferences, a list of ecumenical books, are sufficient. Without the perspective of the ecumenical movement, however, we would be lost. It is a perspective which takes a long view of the achievements which it has wrought, a view indeed which places these achievements in the total perspective of church history. At the same time, it takes a short view of the problems still to be faced, a view set in the immediate and urgent perspective of the street corner.

CHAPTER ONE

❧⸵❧

Where Did All These Churches Come From?

THE WHOLE POINT of Christianity lies in the fact that it influences men's lives. If it did not, we would have none of it. It would be without importance or interest, and no intelligent person would associate himself with it. Whatever our reactions to Christian faith, one thing about it will not let us go. With "majestic beat and constant instancy" there is borne in upon us the knowledge that the course of history, the life of nations, and the life of our neighbor and of ourselves are affected by Christianity. It has to do with people.

This is as important for our personal faith as it is for our understanding of the churches. It goes without saying that a personal faith which makes no difference in life is a mockery. It is perhaps less obvious that the opposite is also true. Our life makes a difference to our personal faith. No two Christians live alike. The New Testament itself shows, in the difference for instance between the writings of Matthew and those of Paul, that Christ meant different things even to those who were very close to him. So with you and me. Our problems are different, our backgrounds are not the same, and our ambitions vary from one another. We approach the eternal truth which is in the gospel from different perspectives and out of varied needs, and its impact upon each of us is therefore different. This is indeed as it was meant to be. Jesus spoke repeatedly of seeds—of how they were planted and affected by the soil, and of how very much like the Kingdom of God this process is. In some soil the seed will not sprout at all; in other earth it will spring up quickly; in still other, it will grow slowly. He never talks specifically about the kind of plant that will come up, but only in very general terms. One suspects that He knew that the plants would be varied, and that their chief characteristics, whatever the flower, would be strength and spreading growth. To think, therefore, only of the flower is to miss the fact that the soil has its influence too; and to think only of the soil is to lose sight of the seed which will grow up through the soil. Christianity and life are all involved with each other.

This means, of course, that the churches are bound up with the life which surrounds them. It is not possible simply to speak of churches as though they existed separatedly from the general environment in which they carry on their work. Pick out any church. It is a church in America. It will not have in it the background of Chinese culture, or British, or German. It will have in it, affecting its organization and activities and life, the background of American culture. It will belong to one of the denominations—Lutheran or Episcopal or Baptist or whatever. So it will share in a tradition which has come down out of the past. It will look to founding fathers and to their ideas as being part of itself and part of its own ideas. But these ideas will never be purely those of the founding fathers; they will have picked up modifications on the way down to the present. A Lutheran Church in Pennsylvania in 1952 is not the same as the Lutheran Church in Wittenberg, Germany, in 1600. And neither is the Methodist Church in Illinois the same as the Methodist group in England which rallied to the preaching of

John Wesley. Moreover, this church will have in it people who, not strictly but on the whole, are people of the same general background and social status. They will all have white skins or brown skins, and thus will all belong to a privileged group or one laboring under severe disabilities. They will mostly be well to do or wealthy; or people who, perhaps with economies, live comfortably within a budget; or for the most part, people who do not have enough to budget but live from day to day. The people in that church will be pretty much alike, and therefore the church itself will be deeply influenced by the dominant characteristics of the people who are its members. It is never purely Christian. It is always Presbyterian Christian, middle-class Christian, Negro Christian, or whatever. The flower is influenced by the soil, and it cannot be otherwise.

If one is to understand the general church situation today, one must bear this fact constantly in mind. The World Council of Churches has within it more churches than any other single agency. There are 160 separate, autonomous denominations, from forty-four different countries. How can you understand these different churches? No one can understand them all; in fact, it is probable that no one can fully understand more than his own church in his own country. We are greatly helped, however, in understanding them and the situation which has brought them about, if we remember that each one is a composite. None is simply the result of the propagation of the ideas of its founding fathers. Nor, on the other end of the scale, is any the mere reflection in religious terms of the culture of its respective nations. Each is basically the response of people to an eternal gospel. As such, each reflects all of the equipment which its members have—equipment supplied by national culture, by political forces, by economic situation, by racial character. It may be regretted that the divisions among those churches seem to be so wide. On the other hand, the very wideness in God's mercy has provided a richness in the structure and tissue of the Body of Christ that is a marvel to those who will appreciate it.

On a narrower scale, the churches in the United States exhibit a similar variety. There are 254 Protestant and Orthodox denominations in the forty-eight states. A host of these are splinters, and they have within them only about 20 per cent of the Protestant and Orthodox church membership. The great percentage, actually about 80 per cent, is found in about thirty churches, and these form a microcosm of the general situation of the churches in the world. The United States itself is an amalgam of the peoples of the world, especially of Britain and the Continent—an amalgam to which, as our European friends hastily point out, have been added some distinctive characteristics in the process of composition. So the United States churches are derived from churches which existed previously elsewhere, chiefly Britain and the Continent, plus churches which have grown up in the American scene.

To understand the American churches, it is necessary to glance briefly at the origins of at least the great families of churches as they exist in the world as a whole. These families may be thought of in five categories: the Lutheran; the Reformed or Presbyterian; the Anglican—or as in America, the Episcopalian; the churches of so-called "free" or "radical" protestantism; and the Eastern Orthodox. With a few exceptions, which we shall indicate later on, American churches all belong to one or another of these groupings. They originated in movements which started long before the American nation was founded; they exist here because they were brought over by those who settled the country and those who added to it through the great immigrations.

I

Our imagination is always caught by an idea which comes at the right time. Well might it be. Nations have been formed and great streams of life have been shaped by the conjunction of a powerful idea with a certain readiness in the affairs of men. Perhaps all of history may be read in these terms: that important things happen when there appears an idea whose time has come. Certainly this was true of the Protestant Reformation. The throbbing movements of human history in the sixteenth century were taking place on the small continent of Europe. Into these movements there came a very few basic ideas.

The first of these ideas was that God's great requirement of man is trust. You do not work your way into the Kingdom of God, and neither, once there, do you earn your keep. God receives us into his kingdom because we trust him. Where does the trust come from? It is given to us by God as we submit to Christ and follow him. It is not a reward, neither is it a thing to be grasped. It is a free gift.

Second, no one stands between man and God. There is no church, no priest, no rule, which can on the one hand lead man to God or on the other keep man away from God. God seeks the human being as he is, and not because he is a member of some group or order or class.

Third, freedom in its deepest and truest sense comes from obeying God. Christian freedom is the result of Christian slavery. As a man is caught by Christ and serves him, thus serving his Father, he becomes free from the influences of pride and ambition which held him before. He knows the freedom of the Christian man.

There were other ideas in the Reformation, but these underlay them all. They are in fact not separable from one another. They are all part of one big idea, which was that God reached directly into human hearts. The Reformation was first and fundamentally a discovery again of the great and simple truth of the Christian gospel.

Why did this cause an explosion? Others before the Reformation had taught the same thing, among them the most Roman of Roman Catholics. Was this idea so new in itself? No clear answer can be given to this question, nor to any other of the imponderable questions in history. Nevertheless some things are clear. There was a deep background of religious faith among the population in general, born out of centuries of church life. Yet there was an almost unthinkable corruption in the popular religion of the day. It was the kind of devilish corruption whereby innocent and ignorant people were deliberately taught, by the representatives of the highest authority they knew, that for money they could buy their way out of purgatory and on toward the way of blessedness; and not only for themselves but for their dear ones who had died. It was a corruption which, through this device and others, drained needed money out of the hands of the people and into the hands of the ecclesiastics for ecclesiastical purposes. It was a corruption in which the most religious, the monks, had sunk into obvious evil. It was a corruption in which the people, among whom a genuine religious restlessness was stirring, were not primarily told of the depth and simplicity of the gospel, but rather of the expensive ritual of the church. To such people, the authority of Luther had a compelling ring: "You are saved by grace alone."

Less wholesome factors played into the spreading reform. Throughout Europe, people were beginning to feel the ties of nation, and to desire the status which a free nation would give

them. Germany in particular was restive, the nobles resenting
rule from an Italian pope and, perhaps even more, chafing
under the financial burden of a great ecclesiastical establishment. The message of Luther against the church, and his
growing following, soon became a rallying point for the cause
of the German nation. The nobles turned for assistance to the
growing mercantile and banking establishments, with the result that economic influence was coupled with political and
religious interest. So the pattern was repeated in country after
country. In England it was somewhat reversed, the political
interests of the British under Henry VIII dictating a break
with Rome, although not the reformation of the church. Deep
religious conviction at a later date, however, coincided with
the conviction of all Englishmen that England must be free
from the domination of foreign princes, especially those of the
Catholic states. In Holland, in the Scandinavian countries, in
Scotland, the great thrust of Reformation ideas coincided with
political and economic developments to establish throughout
northern and western Europe a revolution in the life of nations.

Four great groups of churches resulted. The first was Lutheran, founded in Germany, spreading then to Scandinavia,
and in minorities to Poland and central Europe. Luther did not
wish to form a separate church; he was a monk and at first intended to remain a monk, reforming the church of his faith
from within. He partly led, and was partly driven into the
movement to found a different church altogether. Ultimately,
his ideal for the reform of the Catholic Church settled into the
establishment of Lutheran churches in the countries of northern
and central Europe and, it must be noted, in only part of
Germany. The church reform was widespread: a new and mas-
terful translation of the Bible into German, a new order of worship, marriage of priests, and the abandonment of monasteries

and monastic orders were all involved. More important, however, was the establishment of a new principle of authority.
Previously, the church had been the rule of faith and life for
all men. Now Scripture was substituted for the church, not only
in principle but in fact. The Bible in the vernacular was placed
in homes throughout the land. From it, men derived over and
over again the great principles which Luther had announced:
trust, freely given through faith; the priesthood of all believers; the source of freedom for Christian men.

The second church was the Reformed, or as it is called in
Scotland, England, and the United States, the Presbyterian. It
was found in Switzerland, Holland, central Europe, Germany,
Scotland, England, and France. The founder was Zwingli, but
its great genius was John Calvin, both of whom agreed fundamentally with Luther's main points. At the outset, however, a
difference of conviction concerning Holy Communion established the Reformed as different from the Lutheran. The Reformed, although insisting upon the real presence of Christ in
the sacrament, could not agree with the Lutherans that the
body and blood of Christ existed in the elements along with
the properties of bread and wine. To this difference were added
differences in theological emphasis and in church government,
which tended to be of great importance. The Reformed, under
the great system of doctrine developed by Calvin, centered
their conviction upon the sovereign will of God in Christ, and
although insisting that salvation could not be earned by good
works, nevertheless insisted with equal vehemence that salvation must always be accompanied by good works. In this, there
was no difference from the Lutheran conviction save one of
emphasis, an emphasis shown in the fact that puritanism—an
ascetic kind of life according to strict moral codes—appeared
in the Reformed Church countries rather than in the Lutheran

ones. This overwhelming conviction concerning the sovereignty of God and his righteousness gave to Calvinism and the Reformed churches an extraordinary confidence and assurance in life and in work. On its bad side, the knowledge which the elect of God had of their own salvation led to persecution of those who would not conform. Geneva, Scotland, and New England alike saw cruel acts in the name of righteousness. On its good side, the same quality led men to venture into the day's work with a strong belief that the work itself, so long as it was good and honorable, was a calling from God, and that in pursuing it they were performing their God-given duty.

Church government was of large importance also for the Reformed churches, not only because of the importance attached to the system developed, but because of the effect which it had, initially in Geneva and later in Scotland and the New England colonies, upon civil government. It was a representative system, starting with the governing body of the local church, and proceeding upward to the General Assembly. Laymen and ministers alike participated in it. The General Assembly of Scotland was long a chief force in the life of that nation, and in New England, Calvinist conceptions of church government had a determining effect upon the rule of the colonies.

The third great branch of the Reformation was the Anglican. We have noted that the Reformation first started in England through the political necessities of Henry VIII, who desired a break with Rome and was supported in his policy by rising English nationalism. He did not reform the church internally, this being left to a later date under the influence of a combination of religious and political factors. On the one hand, Protestant ideas had entered England from the Continent, chiefly from Geneva, both directly and through Scotland. On the other hand, it was increasingly necessary that the English

Church and England remain independent from Rome and its entangling Catholic political alliances. Yet a strong Catholic sentiment remained, and no Luther or Calvin emerged to sway the English people. Accordingly, modification rather than outright reform took place in the Church of England. A middle road between the Catholic and the Protestant was maintained, sometimes with deliberate ambiguity. A revised Prayer Book retained much of the ancient, and made modifications according to Protestant conviction, especially in regard to Holy Communion. Monasteries were confiscated and priests permitted to marry, but the bishopric was maintained in the full confidence that the reforms had not broken the episcopal succession. Although the theological position of the church was set forth in the Thirty-nine Articles, which remain definitive, the Prayer Book is more important for the life of the church and the nurture of its members. The Church of England is the mother church of Anglicanism, this general term being used to describe those churches found principally in the countries of the British Commonwealth and the United States which are in full communion with the Church of England and which use the Prayer Book.

The fourth family of churches which developed during the Reformation are the so-called "free churches." This is an ambiguous term, for it is used to cover vastly more churches than those which arose exactly during the time of the Reformation. Certain basic ideas, however, appeared during the Reformation which have, either directly or indirectly, been taken up by other groups, sometimes in places far removed from Europe, with the result that there is an undoubted kinship between the resulting groups and churches. It did not take long for the full implications of some of the basic doctrines of the Reformation to be spelled out, and to be added to some pre-Reformation ideas. A literalist view of the Bible was the most important, the church consisting of those groups which strictly adhered to the law of God in the Bible. From this viewpoint, no other authority is necessary. Moreover, if, as the Bible indicates, one must believe before being baptized, then infant baptism is unwarranted; baptism is a sacrament solely for those who in adult years have reached a responsible decision to serve Christ. The Lord's Supper cannot be thought of in sacramental terms; there is no strict scriptural warrant for such a view. It is a remembrance, a memorial supper, in which Christians gather, to be sure, at the command of their Lord, to do homage to his memory. Here is a "radical" protestantism in which churches, free of great structural and dogmatic systems, rely rather upon the spirit of God and the written word of God alone to unite them.

Held by a rebellious and at first fanatical group, opposed by Lutherans and Reformed alike, this free and radical view was most constructively developed by Menno Simons. The comparatively small Mennonite Church is today his chief direct descendant. But his ideas were not confined. Groups of Baptists grew up in Holland, and from there spread to England. Calvinist Christians in England, impatient with the general strategy of waiting for reform within the Church of England, separated themselves out of the general group of Calvinists, for which they received the name of Separatists, and formed their own congregations, for which they received eventually the name of Congregationalists. Some of the Baptist groups in Holland were basically Calvinist, but took over certain key ideas of the radical elements in the Reformation, especially concerning believer's baptism; and the English Congregationalists, who adopted the radical ideas of the primacy of the congregation, were also originally Calvinists. Here then is a mixture of so-called "classical" and so-called "radical" or "free" protestant-ism.

Less direct descendants of this protestantism have appeared. Of particular importance are both the Quakers, or Friends, and the Methodists, both it will be noted very different in ori-gin and ultimate effect, but both espousing certain fundamental concepts which place them among the "free churches." Quaker-ism arose in England through the experience and work of George Fox, who, as a result of his own religious experience, understood Christianity as the dawn and following of an inner light, a sense of direction and power created in the human heart by Christ, a light sufficient for salvation, leading people into lives of love and mercy in the interests of their fellow men. Methodism, not originally intended to be a separate church, was founded by John Wesley, who saw in Christ the power to enter into the human soul, there to transform and perfect it in works of love and justice. Both groups, though widely different in outward form, in point of time of their origin, and in subsequent history, have at their root a convic-tion of the inner transforming power of Christ; both under-stand that the church is made up of those who freely gather, yet under the compulsion of Christ, because of their common apprehension of the truth.

Common to all of the "free churches" is their attitude to-ward the state. The single exception may be the early New England Congregational practice, where force of circumstance and a basic Calvinism alike tended to make the church the center of the civil state as well. The other groups, and soon after the early days the Congregationalists as well, have in-sisted upon the freedom of the church from the state. In some cases, as with the Mennonites and the Quakers, this has taken the extreme form of non-co-operation with the state in certain matters, especially war. In present-day America, "classical" protestantism, Anglican and Lutheran and Reformed, all insist upon the independence of the church from the state. It was, however, from the first a part of the very genius of "free" protestantism to separate church and state from one another.

From the "free churches" we turn to what is in many ways their opposite. Eastern Orthodoxy, the correct name for which is "the Orthodox Church of the east," is found in different places and in different over-all forms of organizations. The major bloc is composed of the great national churches, each independent, in Russia, Greece, and the Balkan countries. Second, each of the four ancient patriarchates of Constantinople, Alexandria, Antioch, and Jerusalem has under it other groups of Orthodox. Third, are the ancient, self-governing Churches of Cyprus, Georgia, and Sinai. Fourth, Orthodox are found in western Europe and the United States, where they exist chiefly by virtue of immigration, and in the Far East, where they have been created through missionary work. Although there is no single head of these churches, and no over-all organization, they form a loose federation, and are bound together by ties of theology, liturgy, and common history.

What caused the ancient division which separated the Eastern churches from the West? There is no single, concrete answer. Various powerful factors were at work from the fourth century until the thirteenth, when the break was complete. The basic interests and moods of two ancient worlds played against each other. The interest of western Christians in administration, law, and morals differed from the concern of the Greek-speaking churches for doctrine and worship. The prolonged political struggle between Constantinople and Rome affected the churches which had their centers of power in those capitals. Theological differences, especially concerning the nature of the

Trinity, as well as questions of ecclesiastical and liturgical practice played their part. The process was long, involved, and bitter, coming to a final completion with the excommunication of the Patriarch of Constantinople in the eleventh century by the Bishop of Rome, and with the sack of Constantinople by the western Crusaders some two hundred years later.

Eastern Orthodoxy is identified through its theology and its liturgy and by its history. It does not have a single creed, but subscribes to the creeds and theological statements of the seven ecumenical councils. These are regarded as dogmas, that is, as being essential to the Christian life. To these are added the testimonies which define the attitude of Orthodoxy to the Protestant and Roman Catholic churches, and catechisms which are in effect doctrinal summaries. The tradition of the church is of immense weight and importance, and is shown perhaps most vividly to the outsider in the liturgy. The Eastern Orthodox Church regards itself as the true Church of Christ, but this does not prevent portions of that church, as for instance the Church of Greece, from entering into fellowship with other churches.

II

These are the roots out of which American Christianity has come. They are, however, only the roots. In each case—Lutheran, Reformed, Anglican, "free" or "left-wing," Orthodox— the origins of the churches have been inextricably mixed with the influences of national culture. As the churches grew and developed within their native lands, environment continued to make its impact upon deep-seated conviction. Any church history, whether of the Lutheran Church in Germany or of the Church of England, or any other, would have to be written to show the condition of the church during successive stages of the national life no less than the basic ideas which started the church. The same is true of American Christianity. These churches, started in Britain and on the Continent, were transplanted here by people who immigrated. Yet as they settled and developed, an American culture began to arise. The churches they brought with them were affected by this culture, and continue to be. The seed is the same seed, namely the eternal gospel; but as in Europe, so in America, the soil has affected the growing of the plant.

All five of the great branches of the Protestant and Orthodox churches have been transplanted to the United States, originally through immigration. Indeed, the great central bloc of Christianity in the United States, exclusive of Roman Catholicism, consists of denominations which are part of these great families. In accounting for the multiplicity of denominations in the U.S.A., we must remember that within each family there are a number of distinct, separately organized, and autonomous denominations. Thus in addition to the Protestant Episcopal Church,* there are twenty-one Lutheran churches, thirteen Reformed or Presbyterian bodies, twelve Eastern Orthodox; the remainder, nearly two hundred, come under the head of the "radical" or "free church" branch of protestantism. What has caused these numbers? In part, and perhaps the largest part, national origin is responsible. Thus, Lutherans from Germany, Denmark, Norway, and Sweden have formed separate churches here; Reformed from Holland and Germany and Presbyterians from Scotland, Orthodox from Russia, Greece, Hungary, Romania, have done the same. In part, theological difference has

---

* A very small Reformed Episcopal Church (membership about 9,000), created by a withdrawal from the Protestant Episcopal Church, also exists, but in size and influence is not comparable to the Protestant Episcopal Church.

accounted for many denominations, particularly the smaller ones. Offshoots from larger churches have been common, with the result of separate churches which, however, hold almost the same beliefs. Thus, there are thirteen churches in the Reformed or Presbyterian group, twenty-four in the Baptist group, twenty-three in the Methodist group. Racial factors, as well as the influences of sectionalism, particularly the differences between North and South, have added to the divisions.

Some new churches have been formed, many of them around a particular article of Christian doctrine, especially, belief concerning the return of Christ. An especially significant new church, belonging by tradition and present life to the main, central stream of Christianity, is the Disciples of Christ. Although now found in many countries, through missionary work, its origins were in the United States, and its chief strength lies here as well. Originally formed out of a general Presbyterian matrix, the founders and their descendants have held to four cardinal tenets: the absolute supremacy of the Scriptures; a desire for unity among all Christians, providing that this unity is founded on the Scriptures without reference to a creed; the baptism of people who consciously believe, as distinguished from infant baptism; and a congregational form of organization. The Disciples were founded amid the conditions of the frontier.

The influence of the frontier on American Christianity is seen in other ways than the formation of the Disciples of Christ. Methodists and Baptists alike grew in well-nigh phenomenal ways on the frontier as it moved progressively westward. The freedom which each stood for, the availability of Christ for any man, the individualism of the Baptists and the organizational adaptability of the Methodists, especially in the use of circuit riders among the frontier communities unable to support a settled minister, were all congenial to the particular spirit of the frontier and the conditions of its life. As a result, these two immense forms of "free" or "radical" protestantism grew apace, and today they form the two largest blocs of Protestants within the United States.

CHAPTER TWO

❧

What Has Christianity in America Achieved by Way of Unity?

A DEFINITE TYPE of Christian unity has emerged out of the complex variety of churches in the United States. Although proposals for church union go back as far as John Eliot, who labored in the deep New England woods in the 1600's as a missionary to the Indians, neither his nor any of a dozen others has caught the imagination of American Christians. One is tempted to wonder why. Is it because our ingrained individualism makes us shy of large, corporate unions? Not wholly, because this same element has not kept us away from great combines in the industrial world. Is it because of the love of our traditions, inherited from the founding fathers? Not wholly, because these traditions have undergone great modifications without fear or protest, and because, also, proposals for the union of churches within these traditions have been met generally with coolness and indecision. Whatever the reason, the development of Christian unity has progressed upon other lines. Since the beginning of the nineteenth century, Christian unity in America has taken the form, not exclusively but on the whole, of *co-operation* among individuals and among autonomous churches. We shall examine the forms of this co-operation later on, and we shall note exceptions to the general process of development. In general, however, co-operation has become the established form of unity among American churches. It is important to note that it has come for the most part out of a great central bloc of Protestant conviction, which, though divided denominationally, possesses a more or less identifiably common mind. The specific form of Christian unity now accepted as established policy has arisen, in other words, out of a very fundamental unity of outlook, held by Christians of different specific beliefs and forms of life and worship. How has it all come about?

I

The creation of the unifying elements of protestantism in America has been the result of different forces, some of which are external to the church and others have their origins within the churches. Here again the seed and the soil have interacted.

We see this process in the development of a common American Christianity, which in final analysis forms the basis of the growth of unity among the churches. One element in this American Christian "mind" has been contributed by the democratic ideal and temper of American life. The influence of Christianity upon the development of democracy and the effect of the flowering of democracy upon the churches are intimate and pronounced. Without tracing the subtleties of this development, we may note simply that during the period of the Revolution and the longer period of the westward advance of the frontier, Christianity in whatever church it was found was strongly shaped by the democratic ideal. Freedom, individualism, equalitarianism, especially as these were all found on the frontier, entered into and were fostered by the centers of Christian life. The stated policy of the separation of church and state, by which was meant not the banishment of religion from the realm but the refusal of the state to grant favor to any one church, in a certain degree established all churches as equals in the sight of the nation's population, and therefore to a certain degree in the sight of these churches themselves. Whatever each church thought of its distinctive role was inevitably modified by the equalitarianism of the national policy. This lack of official support put the churches on their own—as indeed the democratic dream indicated all men should be—and forced them to maintain their own life by the power of their appeal to the rank and file. It is quite true that this freedom tended to permit churches to divide endlessly without fear of persecution, and thus went counter to the immediate interests of Christian unity. In the long run, however, it was far more important that democratic freedom contributed to a basic, common outlook among the churches; for out of this a lasting and effective form of unity could arise.

A part of this democratic ideal, but needing special note, is the stout and pervasive individualism which has persisted within even the relatively authoritarian churches, has flowered in the congregationally organized churches, and has been part and parcel of American culture. This individualism has had a profound effect upon church life, being perhaps the factor most responsible for the large growth in the United States of the "free" or "radical" type of protestantism. It has had a determining effect upon American theology. By throwing responsibility upon the individual, by emphasizing the need for the individual to take initiative, it has provided a climate in which a similar theology could flower but one opposed would find only limited acceptance. Accordingly, American theology has been on the whole humanist and Arminian, centered, that is, upon the dignity of the human being and upon his ability to make a free decision to follow Christ.

An internal development of early origin and long duration was equally formative. From the period beginning in the late eighteenth century and extending to the early twentieth century, revivalism was characteristic of the churches. The first important movement was the Great Awakening, which under the leadership particularly of Jonathan Edwards and George Whitefield, swept the seaboard colonies, and was followed in the 1840's by the Second Great Awakening, which had particular force on the frontier. Later in that century and in the early 1900's, the Moody revivals continued the same influence. Each awakening was marked by a deep religious feeling. The meetings were informal, sometimes running into excessive emotional demonstrations, always emphasizing the reality of personal conversion unto salvation. At their height they were movements of great spiritual power. Their cumulative influence tended to shape a great portion of Christian thinking, across denominational barriers, so that the need for genuine personal experience, the emphasis upon conversion, the warmth and informality of services, and the concept of a gathered church of committed Christians became to greater or less degree a part of the common property of large sections of the Christian population.

Toward the end of the nineteenth century skepticism set in regarding the effectiveness of the revivals, and the demand for sudden conversion began to give way to the importance of the more gradual process of Christian nurture through religious education. Today it is this latter conviction which largely holds sway among the churches. Nevertheless, the influence of the revivals upon the temper of Christian life has been permanent.

One accompaniment of the revivalist form of Christian life was the tendency to disregard the niceties of theology. Coupled with the lack of adequate educational facilities on the frontier, together with the frontiersman's scorn for education, the result has been that only of late has American Christianity shown a substantial interest in theological questions. This may be a contributing factor to the lack of interest in formal unions between the churches, the theological implications failing on the whole to arouse interest.

Growing out of the revivals, indeed made possible in large part by them, was a common conviction of missionary duty and opportunity. American Christianity grew up constantly surrounded by the need for the presentation of the gospel to those outside the church or in danger of being lost to the church. It is one of the very great achievements of the churches that they were able to follow the great movement of population westward, often in the most adverse conditions, and not only hold that population for the church but produce such a Christian vitality in it that the second of the great revival movements was largely found on the frontier. Toward the end of the nineteenth century, missionary interest shifted, the eyes of literally thousands being fastened upon the opportunities in foreign lands. The foreign missionary movement, starting as early as 1810, nevertheless grew most impressively during the late nineteenth and the twentieth centuries, and to this day remains one of the greatest tributes to the vitality and vision of American Christianity. Today, not only is a foreign missionary enterprise running into over forty million dollars annually being sustained, but the churches are involved in repeated evangelistic efforts in the nation itself. The American churches, as such, have thrown more energy, time, and money into evangelism than into any other single effort. This is a common characteristic, or nearly so, of the churches, and wholly common to the bloc of "radical" or "left-wing" protestantism which forms so large a part of American church life. It may be taken as part and parcel of an understanding of the gospel which, in whatever denominational form, is the possession of all.

The main weight of Protestant Christianity, with one notable exception, has had a middle-class flavor. The one exception is the Negro population, always a disinherited portion of the people, but one in which Christianity was proclaimed with striking effectiveness. The Negro churches, however, being all but wholly segregated, have not had an opportunity to bring into the sum total of Christian experience the outlook of their background. The result has been that the heavy majority of the churches have been almost wholly middle class and bourgeois in their outlook, although not so exclusively so in actual membership. As in the case of the influence of democracy, the relationship here is one of both cause and effect. Puritan conceptions of work, vocation, and morality strongly influenced the development of middle-class conceptions; and the growth of the middle class with its virtues of work and thrift and individualism and personal morality, far outstripping the churches in extent, has had its effect upon Christian or church conceptions. Whatever the verdict may be as to cause and effect, church life has been dominantly middle class. Just as no state-favored church has dominated, so no proletarian church has arisen to challenge the main temper. The result is a unity amid the variations of denominational outlook which has been strong and determinative.

With the growth in the nation of acute problems of social justice has come an awakening also in the churches. Anti-slavery, temperance in the matter of liquor, and the injustices attendant upon large-scale industrial life have called forth a strongly similar response from most churches. It must be noted at once that those groups which still hold to the dominant conceptions of the revivalist period do not join in making this response with the main body of churches which have emerged from the immediate influence of revivalism. The social gospel is opposed by the fundamentalists. Nevertheless, there is a general concern for social justice among the majority of churches which indicates a rather commonly accepted temper of mind. Some caution must be used in evaluating it, for one has the uneasy suspicion that this concern has been at times more loud than effective, more a conviction of the leadership of the churches than of the rank and file.

Such has been, and still is, the generally common outlook of American Christianity. The response of Americans to the eternal gospel has been in terms of democracy, liberty, equality, individualism; in terms of vigorous missionary and social responsibility; in terms also of a certain bourgeois outlook upon all of these matters, which in fact has been the characteristic outlook of the country as a whole. This of course does not mean that Christianity in America has been formed by these elements wholly; it means that the seed has grown in this kind of society rather than in a feudal or Hindu or tribal society. But it also means that Christianity in America has a common texture, which in turn has provided the basis for growth of unity among the churches.

The movement toward unity, however, has been urged on by other forces than simply the existence of a generally homogeneous outlook among church members. Although there were stirrings in the direction of Christian unity very early in the history of the country, on the whole the great development has occurred roughly between 1900 and the present. In these eventful years there appeared forces which had a direct bearing upon the pace with which the churches drew together in unity.

One of the most important of these was the growing sense among Christians of self-consciousness as Christians. Things were happening which seriously challenged the Christian faith as such. Controversy did not rage between Baptists and Methodists, as had once been the case; the dispute now developed between Christians and non-Christians. The leading factor was the growth of science and its religion, scientism. Men were everywhere captivated by the achievement of theoretical and practical science. Life was better. It was easy to say that Christian truths and dogmas and practices were outworn. Science had provided so much so quickly that it was easily and convincingly inferred that with a bit more science the good society and the full life would be here in truth. More than this, scientific methods applied to the Bible began to undermine the basis of the Christian faith itself. People found it hard to believe in a pure and simple way in the story of the Creation and the Virgin Birth. Scholars from the German universities, the most respected in the world, began to say, with "proof," that Jesus did not say what the Bible said he said; and some maintained that we know practically nothing of what he did say. Many reasoned that if any part of the Bible is wrong, that is, if Jesus did not say all that he was said to have said, then the whole must be called into question. It was an easy conclusion for a world not yet disillusioned with scientific work, and indeed on the whole captivated by it. The result of this enthusiasm was not so much a new faith which could be precisely defined, but a tremendous preoccupation. People were, and still are to a great extent, simply absorbed with making things. Call it materialism or what you will, the thing which occupied men's minds was the production of goods, the power whether in the form of money or organization which made production possible, and the use and enjoyment of goods. So preoccupied, men's minds had little room for God. Life was increasingly organized without God in the picture, except in a rather benign way which added a certain luster to the contents of the basic scene. People did not forsake the churches. On the contrary, they joined them in ever increasing numbers. But most did not let their church membership interfere with their life or affect it much. Secularism held firm sway.

It did not triumph. Christians reacted to it in two basic ways. A deepening of Christian thought took place, a deepening which is in process now and which has yet far to go. The Christian interpretation of life was no longer an easygoing thing. It had been challenged to its very roots. The doctrines of the church availed little as they stood. Reinterpretation of them in terms of the challenges was needed. Moreover, a new look at the Bible was demanded. All of this began to take place. No organizing force was behind it; the movement, if movement it was, was spontaneous. It was not centered in any one denomination. The strength of the whole effort lay in its striking at the presuppositions of opposing philosophies; in its rigorous examination and restatement of Christian truth; above all, in its fresh attempt to base Christian thought on a sound understanding of the Bible. In addition, Christians reacted to the growing secularism with an aggressiveness of action, especially in the presentation of the gospel to people up and down the land. Evangelistic campaigns were organized, not by fringe groups but by churches themselves; the gospel was preached and explained in reference to the economic life, the racial problem, the realm of international affairs. Pressed by the opposition, Christians began to reach out.

The upshot of the whole process—and we repeat, we are in the midst of it even now—was that Christians began to be increasingly self-conscious of themselves as Christians. Surrounded by an indifferent or hostile atmosphere, reacting to it in terms of fundamental thought and action, they thought more and more of the church as a whole in the world rather than of the prerogatives of a single denomination. Unquestionably, this growing self-consciousness has been an important element in the development of avowed unity among the churches.

So also has been the pressure of disaster. World War I, world depression, and World War II directly and indirectly stimulated Christians to join in closer ranks. The terrible suffering of the nation in the depression forced Christians together to consider the message and the role of the church in regard to social justice. In both world wars, overwhelming need forced united action in chaplaincy service, ministry to the morale needs of the troops, relief, aid for war prisoners. Perhaps even more important, however, was the general atmosphere, during the latter half of the period, of suffering, of bewilderment at the power of the world's evil, of virtual helplessness—an atmosphere which caused Christians to seek each other out, which caused the lesser disagreements to recede in the face of the great human trouble, which gave to everyone more of a sense of being embattled Christians together rather than of being defensive denominationalists set over against each other.

Quite mechanical factors have also contributed to the movement toward unity. Communications have broken down isolation in the churches as elsewhere. This must not be romanticized, but there has been an advantage in the fact that actions become known, positions are reported, people are inevitably brought closer to one another through travel. A quite different factor has also played its role. This is the necessity of having, perforce, to deal with vast organizations which will not tolerate any but a unified approach to them. The universities are a case in point: it is increasingly their policy not to deal with sects, but only with a united group. The Christian forces, if they are to deal with universities, must get together. The government is an even more important instance. So much of life is affected by the government that the churches at point after point must carry on business with it. Yet it will not tolerate a sectarian approach; unity is required here. Still another pressure was added to help produce unity in the churches.

To them all, however, must be added a quite different element. This is the period—from 1900 to the present, as we shall see in more detail later on—when the ecumenical movement had its rise in the world as a whole. In part it originated from the United States. In part it stimulated the development in America. However this may be, in the providence of God there arose at the same time in which other pressures were operating, a great and commanding vision, the ecumenical vision, the vision of one Church of Christ at work in the world. Men began to understand the meaning of unity in Christ, a unity not to be built but to be entered into, a unity not to be admired from afar but a unity which itself made people desire to receive and express it.

II

All of these factors must be borne in mind in any understanding of the growth of unity in the United States. The present drawing together of the churches is not the result of a single move. It is the result of a complex of interaction of forces and events. It is a young flower sprung from a seed in a certain soil. It has been cultivated with different foods, nurtured by different hands. Within it, as in the seed and flower, there has been the indefinable principle of life, which in this case is the eternal gospel.

Out of this matrix, four types of Christian unity have been formed. They do not correspond to the influences we have described which have gone into the general trend toward unity. It is not necessary that they should. The relationship of cause and effect is indirect, not direct. One cannot say that the pressure of disaster, or of secularism, or of external organizations, has created this or that kind of unity among the churches. These various elements have rather created the desire for unity, and this in turn has worked out in distinguishable ways. Of these there are four: the organic union of churches, which though not extensive is important; the association of individuals for common purposes; the co-operation of church agencies; and the co-operation of churches as such.

Proposals for the union of churches go back to the very early days, and have continued to appear until the present. In pre-Revolutionary days, the proposal of John Eliot in New England was matched by the plan of Count Zinzendorff, leader of the pietist German Moravians, for the union of the large number of different churches in Pennsylvania. In the early nineteenth century the Congregationalists and Presbyterians not only proposed but put into effect for a period of nearly fifty years a "Plan of Union," essentially a plan for the joint pursuit of missionary work on the frontier, one of the most thoroughgoing schemes of missionary unity ever put into effect. It was ultimately repudiated by both groups, but not until after a long period of great usefulness in the common task. Four other proposals were made with seriousness, all in the nineteenth century. They arose out of the Lutheran, Reformed, and Anglican churches, the fourth coming from a newly formed group, the Disciples of Christ. The Lutheran, sponsored by the influential and respected Samuel S. Schmucker, and the Reformed, put forth by Philip Schaff, of equal if not greater influence, came eventually to naught as plans; the discussion which they aroused, however, together with the force of the personalities of their respective leaders, had considerable influence in developing the general cause of unity.

The Episcopal proposal, originating with the conceptions of Thomas H. Vail, and culminating in the proposal of William Reed Huntington, is still a live one, and the occasion for a sustained discussion of unity as well as for approaches to churches as a basis for union. As developed by Huntington, adopted by the Convention of the Protestant Episcopal Church and ultimately by the Lambeth Conference—the world gathering of the bishops of the Anglican Communion—it has become known as the Lambeth Quadrilateral. It involves four points, which are in fact the points around which churches in the Anglican Communion today are willing to discuss union with other churches: (1) the Holy Scriptures of the Old and New Testaments, as containing all things necessary to salvation, and as being the rule and ultimate standard of faith; (2) the Apostles' Creed as the baptismal symbol, and the Nicene Creed as the sufficient statement of the Christian faith; (3) the two sacraments ordained by Christ himself, baptism and the Lord's Supper; (4) the historic episcopate.

The challenge of the Disciples of Christ was of a different order. The founder, Alexander Campbell, withdrawing from the Presbyterian Church, set forth a "Plea" for Christian unity. The basis of unity was simply conceived as a return to the truth of the Scriptures, the simplicity of Christian life free from entangling creeds. Union was to be found in the agreement of all men to submit to Scripture, in order that the supreme task of the church, the evangelism of the world, might be carried out.

The New Testament church was the ideal, to be lived out by obeying the commands of Scripture rather than the interpretations of men. Associations of Christians were accordingly formed, and grew rapidly in the simplicity and freedom of the frontier. Although the union of all Christians was not achieved, in actual fact a new denomination being formed, the insistence of the Disciples upon unity and their participation in movements toward unity has been one of their great contributions to American Christianity.

In recent years, there have been a few organic unions of churches. To understand their significance best, one must see them against the background of the types of organic unions which have occurred throughout the world. In this larger scene, there have actually been four different types of organic union. There is that which takes place within confessional lines, as in the case of the union of separate Presbyterian churches in Scotland into one church. Second, there have been transconfessional unions, as in the case of the United Church of Canada in which Presbyterians, Methodists, Congregationalists, and local Union Churches all united. Third, there is the group of Federal Unions, which may be illustrated by the Federation of Swiss Protestant Churches, in which the Federation recognizes the autonomy of the participating churches but acts for them in matters of common interest. Fourth, there is intercommunion, in which churches which do not practice open communion agree to be in communion with one another, as in the case of the Anglican Church of India, Burma, and Ceylon and the Mar Thoma Syrian Church of Malabar. Of these four types, there have occurred in the United States nine unions of the intraconfessional type, three transconfessional unions, no federal unions, and one agreement of intercommunion.

It is clear that the churches in the United States, as elsewhere, have found it easiest to unite within confessional group-ings. Yet it is also clear that there has not been a great enthusiasm for even this form of organic union. Large families of churches still remain divided into separate churches, partic-ularly the Baptists, Presbyterians, and Lutherans.

The significance of the unions which have taken place, however, must not be minimized, and it will be worth while to list them briefly.

1. In 1911, the Northern Baptist Convention and the Free Baptists merged, the title of the Northern Baptist Con-vention being retained, although in 1951 it was changed to the *American Baptist Convention.*

2. In 1917, the General Synod of the Lutheran Church in the United States, the General Council of the Lutheran Church in the United States, and the United Synod of the South formed the *United Lutheran Church.*

3. In 1917, Hague's Norwegian Evangelical Lutheran Synod, the Synod of the Norwegian Evangelical Lutheran Church of America, and the United Norwegian Lutheran Church in America united to form the *Norwegian Church of America.*

4. In 1920, the Presbyterian Church in the U.S.A. and the Welsh Calvinistic Methodist Church united under the title of *The Presbyterian Church in the U.S.A.*

5. In 1922, the Evangelical Association and the United Evangelical Church united to form *The Evangelical Church.*

6. 1924, the Reformed Church in the U.S. and the Hungar-ian Reformed in America united under the title *Reformed Church in the U.S.*

7. In 1924, the Congregational Churches and the Evangelical Protestant Churches united under the title of *Congregational Churches*.

8. In 1930, the Lutheran Synod of Buffalo, the Evangelical Lutheran Synod of Iowa and other States, and the Evangelical Lutheran Joint Synod of Ohio and other States united to form the *American Lutheran Church*.

9. In 1939, the Methodist Episcopal Church, the Methodist Episcopal Church South, and the Methodist Protestant Church united to form *The Methodist Church*.

Three points will be apparent from the above list. First, and most obvious, the total list represents a certain confessional consolidation. It is interesting to note in passing that this has occurred at the time when unity in terms of co-operation among the denominations began to proceed with noticeable pace and effectiveness. Second, in at least two instances, the Norwegian Church and the American Lutheran Church (German background), national as well as confessional affinities have been involved in the mergers. Third, and by far the most important, there was the bridging of sectional and sociological divisions in the merger which created the present Methodist Church. The great division here had been prior to the Civil War over the issue of slavery. To this were added, during the war and in the years following, the differences between the North and South not only on the treatment of Negroes but on other matters involving southern and northern solidarity and sectionalism. The merger has effectively crossed these non-theological divisions, with the result that the Methodist Church is the largest and most geographically comprehensive Protestant church in the nation.

Three mergers have ocurred which cross confessional lines:

1. In 1931, the Christian Churches (a part of the original movement founded by Campbell in his "Plea" for unity) and the Congregational Churches united to form the *Congregational Christian Churches.*

2. In 1934, the Evangelical Synod of North America and the Reformed Church in the United States united to form the *Evangelical and Reformed Church.*

3. In 1946, the Evangelical Church and the United Brethren in Christ united to form the *Evangelical United Brethren Church.*

We should note that two of these unions involved churches, the Reformed Church in the U.S. and the Evangelical Church, which themselves were the result of previous mergers. In addition, it is clear that none of these unions, although they do to some extent cross confessional lines, bridge the most serious divisions between confessions. They all fall into families which are more or less of the same origin and outlook; none involved serious modification of either faith or order.

The single instance of intercommunion is the agreement reached in 1946 between the Protestant Episcopal Church in the U.S.A. and the Polish National Catholic Church in the U.S.A., an agreement, again, within the framework of a general family.

Beyond the early plans of Eliot, Zinzendorff, Schmucker, and Schaff, which we have noted, some ten additional schemes of union have been actively explored and are now suspended. Five of these have been proposals involving unions within the general Reformed or Presbyterian family and not across confessional lines; one has been between Methodist bodies outside of the Methodist Church; and three have involved transconfessional unions, two being of a radical type. Of these three, one is a proposal for a functional union between the American Baptist Convention and the Disciples of Christ, both different in origin but very similar in fundamental outlook. The two more radical proposals have involved, first, the Presbyterian Church U.S.A. and the Methodist Episcopal Church, before its merger with other Methodist bodies; and second, the Presbyterian Church U.S.A. and the Protestant Episcopal Church.

From the record of successes and of failures alike, it is not difficult to conclude that the route of organic union has not been popular. If this were the extent or even the most important part of the movement toward unity, we would be in a difficult position. Fortunately it is not so, and the great expression of unity has come in other ways.

III

Chronologically, the first of three additional main streams of achievement in unity has involved the association of individuals of different churches for specific purposes. For nearly a century and a half there has been an increasing growth of such movements and organizations. Sometimes they are highly organized; sometimes they are quite informal. Their sum total has been impressive, and they have contributed powerfully to the creation of a tangible movement toward unity, as distinguished from a generally recognizable common mind.

These agencies are more easily comprehended by groupings than by a listing of them separately; indeed a list of them all would run into pages of names. They have, however, tended to fall into certain categories of church life and interest. The first category, both chronologically and perhaps in point of importance, comprises the societies organized for the promotion of home and foreign missions, dating from the founding of the American Board of Commissioners for Foreign Missions in 1810. The second group includes societies for educational purposes, both in the limited religious sense and in the field of preparatory and higher education. Third, many agencies have been formed for various issues of social action, from the first which were concerned with antislavery and temperance, to those founded only yesterday in the interests of Christian political action. Fourth, great lay movements, especially the Young Men's Christian Association, the Young Women's Christian Association, and various branches of the student Christian movement, have had a large popularity and influence. Fifth, there have been many groups organized with greater or less formality for the purpose of theological discussion, bridging gaps both of confession and of theological outlook which was not confessionally limited. Sixth, ministerial associations in the villages and towns and cities have sprung up and flourished for purposes of discussion, clearance of programs on common concerns, and mutual understanding.

These legions of associations of individual Christians have had a very wide influence. They have included both laymen and clergy. In many cases, laymen and clergy have been joined in common efforts, as in the missionary, educational, and social action concerns. In other cases, as in the ministerial groups and the Y.M.C.A. and Y.W.C.A., clergy and laymen have met separately. It has, however, been an important aspect of these associations that the total membership of the church, that is, lay and clergy, have in principle and to a large degree in fact been involved together. In all of them, denominational loyalties and affiliations have been secondary, the chief point of each association being the specific cause for which it was organized. The antislavery campaigns gathered Christians of all types together, as have the missionary movements and the others. This is not to say that the significance of the churches has been consciously undervalued. It is to say that in emphasizing a common cause, matters of denominational loyalty have been forced into the background in the interests of that cause. In some cases, regrettably, the particular association has come to take the place of the church for its participants, and in other cases so to minimize the place of the churches as virtually to discount them altogether. This has been the exception rather than the rule, however, and the general temper has been that of work within the life of the churches and for their fundamental interests.

The cumulative influence of these associations, apart from their specific aims, has been heavily in the direction of advancing the unity among Christians and the churches. They have actually brought thousands of Christians together, calling them out of their isolation, focusing their attention upon large and imaginative issues, demonstrating the ability of people to work together for a specific end, even if they differ in matters of deep concern. From one viewpoint this may be open to attack—on the grounds that deep differences have been overlooked in the interests of getting the job done and that therefore the unity created is superficial. On the other hand, there is an unquestioned benefit in the fact that isolation has been broken down, that Christians have begun to understand each other, and that, in consequence, differences of even a profound character are not felt to be necessarily heretical and to be ruled out of court. The difference between the spirit of unity in these associations and the rigid temper of the Puritan community that expelled Roger Williams is in very truth immense. In addition, ideas have been spread through the work of these agencies which have had their unifying effect. We have spoken already of the unity among the churches caused by the commonly recognized missionary responsibility of each. The same holds true of educational concepts and gradually growing convictions of social justice. The development of certain main elements of common theological conviction is still another case in point. Directly and indirectly, the cause of unity has been powerfully set ahead through their work and through their example.

In due course, many of these agencies have been taken into the purview of the churches. Missionary, educational, and social action groups in particular have found their way into the official structure of the churches, although many of them still remain independent of ecclesiastical control. Situated thus closer to the center of church life, these agencies have not lost their significance in the movement for unity, but have, on the contrary, increased their influence.

IV

The third form of unity results from the need of specialized agencies of the churches to co-operate with each other. The fact that the denominations themselves undertook the work of missionary promotion and supervision did not kill off the drive inherent in that work for the achievement of unity. A different form of unity emerged, namely the comprehensive agency which gathered together specialized agencies of the churches, along with voluntary agencies of individuals. This has been a temporary development only, and the most important agencies in this category are already out of existence, having been merged in the formation of the National Council of the Churches of Christ in the U.S.A. They must be stressed, however, as an integral part of the general picture of Christian co-operation, because they brought and still maintain their particular contribution to the whole.

We can best refer to the main agencies in the field, for they were not many and their names will indicate their character. They were the Foreign Missions Conference of North America, the Home Missions Council of North America, the International Council of Religious Education, the United Council of Church Women, and the United Student Christian Council. They were all associations, in the sense that their programs were in no way binding upon their constituent members. They served chiefly as clearing houses, though in some cases they had committed to them common programs of action which they administered on behalf of their constituents. In them were involved both denominational and interdenominational societies; they thus gathered together the chief agencies concerned with specialized functions which, before their founding, had carried on separately. Agencies for social action, so far as they were united, found their focus elsewhere, as we shall explain later. Thus in great areas of Christian concern, from about the turn of the century when the first of these comprehensive agencies was founded, means of understanding, co-operative action were established.

V

The fourth form of co-operation has been various types of federations of churches. In one sense, they have all been a single type; for they have all been built upon the principle of a federation of autonomous bodies, none of which has by virtue of joining the federation relinquished its autonomy. *Council* is a better, and indeed the more popular, word. The variation has consisted in the creation of councils in cities, in states, and in the nation as a whole. The most significant are the city council of churches, and the national council of churches.

It is interesting that the development which has finally become the standard expression of Christian unity in the United States arose not from missions nor from education, those two great concerns of American Christians, but from a concern which in fact did not stir the mass of church membership greatly, but chiefly the leadership of the churches. Local councils and the Federal Council of the Churches of Christ in America alike had their origin mainly in the response of church leadership to the evils of industrial society. The first of the city councils of churches were organized principally to combat in a united way the problems created by industrialism. Although the Federal Council was, as its constitution indicated, organized for the achievement of broad principles, and although the number of church leaders behind the movement was considerable, its main impetus came from those who were principally concerned with the moral life of the nation and the impact of the churches upon the social order.

The development of city councils of churches has been widespread, over eight hundred being at present in existence. The figure is somewhat misleading, for less than two hundred have paid executive leadership, and many are very weak in their influence, even when full-time leadership is available. One reason for this lies in the fact that they are composed of representatives of local churches, which although they may take such common community action as may be desired, are limited by virtue of their denominational ties in the extent to which they may enter into serious discussion and action concerning effective unity. A denomination, acting nationally, can raise even such a far-reaching question as its own merger with another denomination. A single congregation in a given city, however, is bound by denominational policy at all points, and can only tentatively and usually with indifference discuss and act upon them. Sober as a realistic judgment of them must be, however, it is clear that the rapid spread of city councils of churches has established a pattern and a framework—even though feeble—for consultation and joint action among the congregations at the very place where they are most needed. At the present moment, the work of the city council of churches is the place where most ministers and laymen concerned with the thorough development of unity may most readily and fruitfully take hold.

From its establishment in 1908 until its merger in 1950 into the National Council of Churches, the Federal Council of the Churches of Christ in America developed steadily and with increasing influence. Throughout its history it maintained a strong insistence upon the need for bringing the Christian conscience to bear upon problems of social injustice. It was a rallying point for all concerned with the social gospel. Yet it was far more than that. It was the main center for the development of a sense of working unity among the churches. It was the most comprehensive agency on the scene, in the sense that churches as such were its members, rather than the specialized boards or agencies of the churches. It strove constantly to broaden its membership, and by 1950 included the full range of non-Roman churches in the United States: Orthodox, Anglican, Reformed, Lutheran, and "radical" or "left-wing" protestantism. The great omission from its ranks was the Southern Baptist Convention, which, however, participated in the Foreign Missions Conference. Although the Federal Council in its original constitution intended to have local branches, it did not achieve this in a strict organizational sense. A lively working relationship with the growing city councils of churches, each independent, did, however, maintain a fruitful contact with what has come to be called the "grass roots."

In 1950, the National Council of the Churches of Christ in the United States of America was formed, after years of planning and negotiation. It was formed by the expedient, which in theory seems simple but in practice has been extremely complicated, of merging the interdenominational agencies which existed for a special function with the agency which brought together the churches as such. Although some seventeen different agencies have to date been brought into the National Council, its basic formative bodies were the specialized agencies dealing with foreign missions, home missions, religious education, and women's work, and the Federal Council of Churches. It is, as were all of its predecessors, a council, with no more authority over its constituents than those members are willing from time to time to give it. It is not a union of the churches; it is a council of the churches and their agencies. The decisions of a biennial Assembly, large in membership, are administered by a General Board which usually meets bimonthly. The work of the National Council is carried on through four main divisions, foreign missions, home missions, Christian education, Christian life and work, and a host of related departments, of which the chief are the departments of men's and women's work, of overseas relief and interchurch aid, and public relations, broadcasting, and films. The divisions are autonomous within their own fields, but subject to the General Board for any policy or program which affects the National Council as a whole. The National Council, operating for its first two years on an annual budget of over six million dollars, is a large organization and complicated in its mechanism.

Three points of particular importance concerning the National Council must be emphasized. First, it is comprehensive, organizing into a single unit the various previously existing agencies which were concerned—on a national basis—with Christian co-operation. Second, it is fundamentally a council of churches, responsible to the churches and engaging them in its business. Third, it combines with this fundamental responsiveness to the churches a means whereby the special agencies and boards of the churches may co-operate with each other, within a whole rather than through separate agencies. In this fashion, the National Council, which is a daring venture in Christian co-operation, combines the sharpness of special interest with the comprehensiveness of full-scale interchurch co-operation.

It is too early to offer any kind of evaluation of the National Council of Churches, but it is not too early to say in some measure what the fact of its founding represents. It has been rightly spoken of as the climax of the ecumenical work in the United States of half a century or more. But in what sense? The sheer fact of its creation is testimony to the depth, range, and power of ecumenical conviction. The National Council is large; the Federal Council in the year of its founding, 1908, was miniscule. The National Council has stated interests ranging from the translation of the Bible to Christian broadcasting and film production, from a chaplaincy service in the national parks to missionary work in the far reaches of the earth. The National Council gathers into one, albeit extremely complicated, agency the churches, their specialized boards and agencies, and more informal groups of Christians who are organized in one or another ecumenical concern. This has never been possible before. Prior to 1950, ecumenical people desired to work separately in a dozen different interdenominational agencies among which there was no co-ordination, much less unity. Prior to 1950, the churches as such worked together in one way; their foreign boards in another agency; their boards of education in still another; their boards of home missions in a yet different group. Interdenominational work was so organized as almost to pull the structure of the churches apart into separate agencies, rather than to encourage their unity within themselves and among each other. This is the organizational and structural way of pointing to what is undoubtedly the deepest significance in the founding of the National Council. This single, ecumenical agency at root stands for the fact that the entire range of interest in the ecumenical movement is relevant to and must become part and parcel of the life, the thinking, and the work of the churches themselves. Ecumenical Christianity cannot be something apart from the church and the churches. It must be in the center of their life. To this, the founding of the National Council is a vivid testimony. It bears out the fact, also, that ecumenical Christianity has taken root in the American scene in a way which cannot be denied. Fifty years ago this structure, this range of interest, this participation by virtually the total life of the churches, simply could not have been possible. There was not the conviction to sustain it. Now there is. It is too much to say that any specific organization, the National Council or any other, is a part of the plan of work of the Holy Spirit. But it is not too much to say that God wills a growing unity in his church, and that there is in the churches a growing response to this will. The drive to unity among Christians is a work of the Holy Spirit. It is a powerful work, on the march. The National Council is a convincing sign of the work of the Holy Spirit in this respect among American Christians.

It is thus clear that the highway of unity in the United States has taken a clear and well-defined direction. It runs squarely across the land of co-operation, with only a second-class road into the areas of union. The traffic upon it, once consisting only of the light vehicles of individual associations, has increasingly become the heavy-duty load of official churches. The one might run the faster, but the other carries more weight. Can the highway stand the load? We shall return to this question in the last chapter, but let us indicate here that this is not quite the proper question. The highway as it is may not stand the load; but it can be strengthened and rebuilt, and thus can be made to stand a load which has not yet even begun to appear. The real question is: Shall it be broadened and strengthened, or rebuilt along a different route?

CHAPTER THREE

❧§❧

What Are Our Agreements and What Are Our Differences?

WE SHIFT OUR ATTENTION to the world scene, because it is on this wider scale that our agreements and differences may most reliably be seen, and because here we have some objective authority for indicating what they are. The common mind of American protestantism and the predominance in it of "free" or "radical" protestantism make it difficult to appreciate the full impact within the Christian community of the more pronounced traditions of "classical" protestantism, Anglicanism, and Eastern Orthodoxy. These traditions are all to be found in America, but either so modified or in such a minority as to make an appreciation of them difficult. Moreover, it is on the world scene that the most careful and authoritative attention has been given to agreements and differences alike. The great world conferences of the past twenty-five years, especially those concerned with the faith and the order of the churches, have provided the objective basis upon which to make an estimate of our present position.

I

Is there a common message which the churches can present to the world? Can we say anything together, and if so what is it? If one carefully scrutinizes the great statements of the recent world conferences on the faith, the statements of the Lausanne Conference on Faith and Order of 1927, the statements of the Edinburgh Conference on Faith and Order of 1937, the Madras message on the faith of 1938, and the Amsterdam statement of 1948, one discovers that there is a very great deal that the churches have said together. This gospel upon which all agree touches the four cardinal points of Christian theology. Common affirmations are possible concerning God, the person and work of Jesus Christ, the condition of man, and the nature and function of the church. The following paragraphs summarize the message of the churches on these matters, being based upon the statements indicated above, all of which were adopted unanimously by their respective meetings.

God, who created and rules the world, is sovereign. His all-controlling, all-embracing will is supreme over each person and over the destiny of the human race. God is love, and in fulfilling his righteous purposes among men and in the world, he acts out of love. Our creation, preservation, and all of the blessings of our life, above all the redemption of men in Christ, are the result of God's love toward the world. God is the giver of Jesus Christ, having prepared the world for the coming of Christ. God is the source of man's welfare and salvation.

Jesus Christ, who is the eternal word of God, incarnate and made flesh at once divine and human, is the unique revelation of God to men. We know God by virtue of knowing Christ.

Christ forgives our sins, and reveals the fullness of God, which is his boundless love for men. Through his life and teaching, his call to repentance, his proclamation of the coming of the Kingdom of God and of judgment, his suffering and his death, his resurrection and exaltation to the right hand of the Father, and by his sending of the Holy Spirit to be with us always, Christ accomplishes his work of forgiveness and of salvation. By the appeal of his love, which we see supremely upon the Cross, he summons us to be his disciples. Jesus Christ is the Head of the Church, and as the Head of the Church he is present in it as the Prophet, proclaiming the will of God; the Priest, offering intercession for us, as he sacrificed himself for us upon the Cross; and as King, ruling and establishing and extending his kingdom.

Man is a child of God, created by God, made in his image. Through freedom, itself a gift of God, man has chosen to serve other gods and has become a law unto himself, looking for salvation where salvation cannot be found. He is sinful, in need of forgiveness, subject to death, suffering, and injustice of his own making. Yet he is capable of a new life, a new life given through faith in Christ, a life of trust, self-sacrifice, devotion, deliverance from sin and from death. He does not earn this new life; it is not given to him through any merit of his own. He is saved out of his miserable condition by God's love which brings man back to God and his righteousness. God's love is known through faith, but this faith, which is an attitude of trust and acceptance, not merely intellectual belief, is itself a gift of God. Man is a free creature, yet at the same time he is subject to the sovereignty of God. The philosophical contradiction involved in this freedom and this subjection is not resolved nor is its solution regarded as a part of Christian faith.

The church is the People of the New Covenant, the Temple

of God, the Body of Christ, the Household of God. Christ is
the head and God is the creator of the church; it is not created
through man's efforts. It is in the church that men are recon-
ciled to God as the Holy Spirit awakens faith and trust in their
hearts, faith and trust in Christ through whom men know God.
It is in the church that the wills of men are brought into subjection to God's will, that they are made holy and righteous in
life as they make use of the means of God's grace. The church
is One, Holy, Catholic, and Apostolic in its character.

The church is recognized in the world by different marks.
The church possesses the Word of God as this is given in the
Scriptures and is interpreted to individuals and to the community by the Holy Spirit. It is composed of those who profess faith in God as he is incarnate in Jesus Christ. The church
is the community which accepts the commission of Christ to
preach the gospel to all men. In the church the sacraments are
observed. The church possesses a ministry, which has been
divinely appointed and authorized by Christ, a ministry which
has pastoral duties, and to which the preaching of the Word
and the administering of the sacraments are entrusted. The
church is a fellowship in prayer, worship, and in the use of
the means of grace. The sacraments are divinely appointed and
are a very part of the church, not standing alone by themselves, but rather belonging to the church in the sense that it
is the Holy Spirit which both creates the church and works
through the sacraments for the salvation of men. The sacraments are both an outward sign and an inward grace; they are
the means of God's grace, but that grace of God is not confined
to the sacraments. In Holy Communion, which is the most sacred act of worship of the church, men have fellowship with
God in Christ; Christ is present in Communion. It is an act in

which the Lord's death is both proclaimed and commemorated, a sacrifice of praise and of thanksgiving.

The function of the church is to glorify God in its life and in its worship, to proclaim the gospel to all men, and to build up a fellowship of every race and nation and class. It is called to make its members, through the ministry to them of the Word and the sacraments, convinced Christians, conscious of their salvation; it is to provide pastoral care for their needs; it is to proclaim the righteousness of God and to fight ceaselessly against evil in the world.

The Kingdom of God is found wherever men obey the will of God. In its fullest sense, however, the Kingdom of God is still to come, for it is realized now only in a dim and veiled form.

These, so far as one is able to reproduce them in this form, are the great convictions of the Protestant, Anglican, and Orthodox churches alike. This is what Christians in Europe, America, Africa, and the Orient believe. If one wanted to know the very kernel of the Christian faith, that which the churches could all present to the outside world, one would point to these basic convictions.

One can also point to a common Christian action. Prior to 1948, the churches of the world met and acted together only at infrequent times and without any regular process. World conferences of duly appointed delegates from the churches were held from time to time; various agencies were created which brought people from the churches together on a world-wide basis for specific reasons. We shall have more to do with this development in a later chapter, for it is of great importance. Yet none of these conferences or movements prior to 1948 demanded any permanent commitment on the part of the churches

as such. At that time, however, such a commitment was asked
for and received. Delegates from 148 churches, who were
empowered to do so by their churches, created a World Council of Churches.

What is this World Council of Churches? We shall deal with
its more external characteristics in a later chapter. Here we
are concerned to indicate what the World Council of Churches
represents, as it were, in the development of the history of the
Christian church, and to suggest that in the realm of action,
that is, of commitment made by the churches, it is in a sense
parallel to the common message which the churches can present together.

The World Council of Churches is a council, and it is composed of churches. As a council, it has no authority over its
constituent member churches. Its authority is wholly moral,
and in this lies a part of its true significance. This is to say that
the World Council has influence according to the intrinsic
weight of the truth which its statements and actions may contain. Its authority does not rest upon coercion of any type, except the coercion of truth. Its deliberations, its actions, and its
programs are effective only insofar as they make an impression
upon the Christian mind and conscience of its members. It is
thus, in the sweep of church history, the modern development
of the ancient conciliar theory of church government. That
theory involved the power of the council over the constituent
parts. The conciliar theory embodied in the World Council
does not involve power, but provides a structure within which
statements and actions may be arrived at in common and may
make their own impact upon the churches. As one speaks of
the World Council, it must be remembered always that it is a
council of churches; there is no substance to the World Council, or for that matter any true council of churches, except the

substance provided by its members. Reduced to its most basic form, therefore, the World Council is the permanent framework within which the churches may arrive at common positions and carry through common programs of action. These common positions and actions stand and are effective by virtue of such intrinsic authority of truth as they may be given by the Holy Spirit.

The World Council is therefore in no sense a superchurch. It is not a Protestant Vatican. It cannot force any member to do what that member does not want to do, nor to believe what it does not want to believe. The World Council cannot negotiate unions among churches. Neither is it able nor does it try to advocate any one theory of church unity. It does not push forward any particular means by which the churches can achieve greater unity.

Nevertheless, the World Council is a structure in which churches have made a commitment to stay together. If the fact that the World Council rests upon moral authority only is the first point in its fundamental significance, the commitment made by the churches to stay together is the second. This commitment, made by *churches*, has profound implications. It means that any one and all of the 148 churches, by agreeing to join with other churches, thereby recognize those other churches in some sense to be churches. It does not mean that every one must recognize the others as full and true churches. It does mean, and it has been explicitly recognized that it does mean, that in some sense every member church recognizes every other member church as a church. To our American ears this may sound quite platitudinous, for on the whole the churches in America take for granted that other denominations are churches. It is not so in the world at large however; the greatest problems in unity center around the fact that many churches consider themselves to be the only true and full church. The mutual recognition of each other as in some sense constituting what may be legitimately called churches, whether Quakers, Baptists, Anglicans, or Orthodox, means that the greatest barrier, the deepest source of isolation, has been broken down. In some sense, all churches meet each other on common ground. Moreover, disunity has been caused at an equally profound level by the conviction of some churches that they alone have a unique relationship to the One, Holy, Catholic church. These churches continue in this faith, even as members of the World Council; and membership in the World Council, as has been explicitly stated, does not imply that they must give up this faith. Yet it is also recognized that whatever a church thinks of its own relationship to the universal church, the relationship of other churches to the universal church is an open and not a closed question. This means in effect that no church in the World Council is of such a closed mind that it rules other churches out of the universal church. A basis is thus provided for the development of further unity among them all. The commitment to stay together in the World Council has provided implications for the churches' relationships with each other, and for their relationship to the church universal, which are of the greatest magnitude. The full meaning of these implications is by no means clear; discussion of it has only begun. The fact, however, that it is discussed indicates the immediate awareness of the churches of the significance of what they have done in creating a World Council of Churches.

II

If there is a common faith, if there is a common framework of commitment and action among the churches, and if this opens up room for greater unity, why does not the movement proceed apace? What holds us back? Is it simply because we do not know what form, beyond the present association in the World Council of Churches, further unity should take? Or is the matter deeper?

The matter is very much deeper. It is deeper than the affirmation of a common message, important as that is. It is more fundamental than the establishment of a common frame of consultation and action. The further development of Christian unity is hindered by three fundamental factors:

> Within the general agreement about the nature of the church, there still are disagreements which seriously affect the life and functioning of the churches, and which are barriers to unity.
>
> There are profound differences of perspective upon the totality of the faith.
>
> There are differences which, arising in the world at large, encroach upon the church, dividing it as they divide the world.

Underneath the agreement which we have already noted concerning the nature and function of the church, there are disagreements which strike to the depths of both thought and action. Five are of pressing importance.

1. There is a difference of conviction regarding the relation of the church to the Kingdom of God. Many Christians stress the fact that the church and the Kingdom of God are akin, that in the church the Kingdom of God is already to be seen, and that in building up the church we are also building up the Kingdom of God. Others see rather the vast distinction between the Kingdom of God and the church, feeling that the Kingdom can be known only through faith and that it will come in glory

through the victory of Christ at the end of this age. If the first view is held, man's hopes will be different from what they will be if the second view is in mind. Hope will center in the eternal power of the church, and it is there that they will be realized; whereas according to the second view, hope for the Kingdom of God must be deferred until it comes at the end of time. There is difference, moreover, concerning the importance of the whole matter: some feel that difference of opinion on this point is not a real barrier to the union of the churches; others feel that it is a deep and serious obstacle.

2. What is the relation of the visible church to the invisible church, and indeed, is it scriptural and right to think of the invisible church at all? Some hold that "church" rightly refers both to the visible community of the redeemed and to the invisible church; others hold that this is not a scriptural description of the church, and that the church must be thought of as visible. The difficulty with the first view, which includes the invisible church in the definition, is that it could be construed to mean that a visible church is not necessary or that the visible church is not true. The difficulty with the second view, which says that the church is visible only, is that it does not provide for the possibility—and the reality—of salvation outside of the church.

3. Some believe that the membership of the visible church includes all of those who are baptized, and some believe that the true membership of the church consists only of those who consciously profess faith in God as he is revealed in Christ. This is a difference which has large historical and social implications. The one is the view of the comprehensive church which welcomes all who are brought to its doors for baptism and works in order that they may all be developed into faithful Christians. The other is the view of the small, gathered group

of convinced Christians who have made conscious decision for the Christian faith and who exclude those who have not reached this point.

4. Great difference of opinion centers around the sacraments, the weight of which is the more appreciated when it is recalled that common conviction holds that the sacraments are the means of the grace of the Almighty God, and that the Holy Communion is the most central and holy act of worship in which Christians engage. Differences of conviction exist on three points, and become extremely acute on two additional matters. First, there is disagreement on whether the sacraments are necessary to salvation, and this disagreement, it will be recognized, is related to the discussion as to whether or not all of the redeemed are to be found within the visible church. If the sacraments are necessary to salvation, the redeemed are to be found where the sacraments are, namely, in the church. If men may be redeemed outside of the visible church, the sacraments become in principle not necessary to salvation. Second, there is disagreement as to whether there are properly seven sacraments, as the Orthodox believe; or whether there are but two, as most Protestants believe. Third, there is disagreement concerning the sacrament of baptism, whether it is properly to be administered to infants and adults or adults only. This in turn is related to the disagreement concerning the membership of the visible church. The churches which hold to the comprehensive principle of membership are churches which practice infant baptism; churches which feel that the members of the church must be consciously committed Christians are on the whole churches which baptize adults only.

A serious and pressing difficulty, which cannot be fully analyzed here, is responsible for the original division of some of the churches, and it remains a stubborn obstacle to further unity. It concerns the way in which Christ is present in Holy Communion. No one doubts his presence in the Eucharist. But as to the way in which he is present—whether directly through the bread and wine and if so in what fashion, or whether in spirit as Christians gather to commemorate his death—these are matters of deep difference.

An equally serious and perhaps even more far-reaching difference concerns the validity of the sacraments. The problem is how to determine whether the sacrament is a really true and valid one. This in turn is a question as to the authority by which the sacrament is administered in the name of Christ. Does anyone have this authority, and if not, who does have it, and by what right? This question directs attention to the authority of the minister who administers the sacrament. Some feel that the validity of the ordination of the minister who administers the sacrament determines the validity of the sacrament. All are agreed that the personality of the man who administers the sacrament has no bearing upon its validity; but many hold that the authority by which he has received ordination as a minister of the Church of Christ affects the authority by which he administers the sacrament. If the authority underlying his ordination is defective, the authority by which he administers the sacrament is defective and its validity is impaired. Others do not believe that the ordination of the minister is relevant to the problem at all, and while they would not have difficulty on this point, they constitute a difficulty for those who believe that the authority of ordination lies at the root of the whole matter. This constitutes only part of the difficulty and leads us to the next point.

5. Perhaps the most stubborn difficulty lies in differences of conviction concerning the authority of the ministry. All are agreed that the ministry must stand in a recognizable succes-

sion of the church from the time of the Apostles down to the present. But what kind of recognizable succession? Some believe that this must be a succession of bishops who ordain ministers by the laying on of hands. Two points are involved here: the passing of the succession down through the act of the laying on of hands on those to be ordained, and the continuous existence of bishops as guardians of the faith and pastors of ministers. Others regard the presbyters, or the presbyteries as the groups themselves are called, as the vehicle through which the apostolic succession is handed down, the laying on of hands at ordination being done in the name of the presbytery. Still others regard the apostolic succession as being correctly passed through the centuries by the faithful congregation which witnesses to the Word of God. It is this group which possesses authority to ordain ministers. As we have seen in other instances, we have here again a situation in which a difference of conviction becomes compounded by affecting other matters over which there is also a divergence of opinion. The different conceptions of apostolic succession define different conceptions of the authority of the ministry, which in turn define different conceptions of the validity of the sacraments. Unity is impeded by both difficulties.

This is the point, we may incidentally point out, which makes the problem of intercommunion such a thorny one. Who is to administer communion to the members of the mixed or different congregation? Is he to be one ordained by a bishop, a presbytery, or a congregation? If he is one ordained by a presbytery or congregation, the sacrament which he administers will not be valid in the eyes of those who look to the bishop. If he is one ordained by a bishop, he cannot give the sacrament to any except church members confirmed by a bishop, and he will find objections raised by the other groups because he insists upon his right alone to administer a valid sacrament. It may be that a minister ordained by a congregation will not be recognized in full right by other congregations, because those other congregations will not regard the congregation out of which the minister has come to have truly kept and witnessed to the Word.

These five points of difference all exist underneath a common agreement concerning the nature of the church. To them must be added an even more troublesome factor, namely, the existence of a totally different approach to the doctrine of the church, even to the whole of the Christian faith, held by different groups within the Christian community. One of the great contributions of the Amsterdam Assembly in 1948 was to bring out clearly that such a difference in orientation and outlook does in fact exist, and is responsible for many of the smaller points of difference within the church. In so doing, Amsterdam brought into the open a fact that had begun to be felt earlier. At the Faith and Order Conference in Edinburgh in 1937 it was said that "we are led to the conclusion that behind all particular statements of the problem of corporate union lie deeply divergent conceptions of the church."

Feeling its way, and lacking in precise terminology, the Amsterdam Assembly defined these different viewpoints as the "catholic" and the "protestant." Those at the Assembly and many since have expressed their dissatisfaction with those terms, but for want of better ones they must be used. They are meant to indicate not two distinct churches, nor in a wholly precise fashion even two groups of churches. They are rather meant to indicate two typical, coherent ways of looking at the Christian faith, which are roughly adopted by different groups of churches. It was readily recognized that many in both groups would want to affirm much that is held by the other. Precision of definition is not, however, of great importance. The discovery of Amsterdam was not a formula. The new light was thrown upon the existence of two systems of approach to the Christian faith, two orientations which in fact color all of the particular agreements and all of the particular differences that exist among the churches.

A somewhat illuminating description of these two viewpoints was provided by the Edinburgh Conference in 1937. The one, they said there, is more authoritarian in its outlook, regarding the church as something which in an absolute sense is *given* to us by God. It is given to us, rather than fashioned by us, in the Scriptures, as well as in the orders of the church and in the creeds and in worship. It is a reality into which we enter, and in a sense, to which we submit. The other is a more personal view of the church. It emphasizes more strongly the individual experience of God's grace; it looks to the more conscious, tightly knit fellowship of Christians—the more closely gathered church. In it men enjoy freedom as a right and practice it as a religious duty.

The terminology of Amsterdam was better, though it pointed to the same reality. The "catholic" view of the faith and of the church refers consistently to the visible continuity of the church in the apostolic succession of the episcopate. Put in other language, this view thinks of the continuity of the church as a horizontal line stemming from the Twelve whom Christ appointed, and reaching to the present. It is a view which identifies the visible church more closely with the invisible church, and which is inclined to desire the unity of the church in visible and structural, rather than purely spiritual, terms. It would hold that the Scriptures and the tradition of the church are involved with each other, and in one form or another are dependent upon each other. It emphasizes the priestly function of the ministry in the offering of intercession and in the sacrifice of the Eucharist.

The "protestant" view differs at every point. The continuity of the church is seen to consist, not in the historic episcopate, but rather in the initiative of the Word of God and the response of the faithful through the ages. It thinks not so much of a horizontal line reaching to the Twelve appointed by Christ, but of a vertical relationship with the living Lord of the church. Not intent upon structure, this view holds that the church is to be found where the Word of God is rightly preached and the sacraments are rightly administered. The unity of the church rests not upon a visible structure, but rather upon the faithfulness of the witnessing congregation. Scripture is always supreme over tradition, acting as the norm and standard of judgment for the tradition of the church. The priestly function of the ministry is less in view, and the priesthood of all believers is a more central conviction.

It is agreed by all that vastly more work needs to be done before the distinction is wholly clear between these two viewpoints. The chief difficulty is that many in both groups would affirm what is here claimed for one or the other. Nevertheless, it is clear that a line of thinking has been started which promises to be very fruitful. One of the greatest difficulties in the whole movement toward unity is to see the true differences, and to see them in proper perspective. It so frequently happens that the real problem seems to be in sight, only to slip away in misunderstanding. The knowledge that many lesser differences must be seen within the context of two different systems of Christian thought and practice gives hope that we may soon be able to discuss the basic realities of our situation, seeing them clearly for what they are, and thus be led into an even greater understanding than exists at present.

From differences which concern the faith of Christians and the churches, we turn to differences of quite another kind. These are the differences which, appearing in the world at large, work their way into the churches, separating Christians there as they have separated men in the world. In speaking of the differences of faith, we have been in fact speaking of divisions—differences, that is, which keep Christians apart from each other. The fellowship which exists at conferences and in committee rooms is always haunted by the fact that it is shattered at the Lord's Table, where we cannot all meet together, and by the fact that we do understand so little of the depth of each other's thinking. In this sense we have not been speaking of mere variations of opinion and practice, for these are to be expected and welcomed. The same is true of variations which result from national and psychological and cultural differences among us. In some cases they have kept the churches apart. Increasingly, they no longer do so—with one great exception to which we shall have reference—but rather provide a richness of background which is to be welcomed, though it may present its difficulties. Some of these variations are, to be sure, important obstacles in the way of achieving the organic union of the churches. But organic union is a much debated goal, and we are not at this point concerned with it. We are thinking of something much deeper.

Writing in the white heat of the racial situation in South Africa, Alan Paton has put the matter in these words: "What we dread about separation is not residential or territorial separation, or the existence of separate congregations in Parktown and Orlando, or the provisions of separate hospitals and churches and schools, but the profound separation of man

from man." The lesser separations are important, as Alan
Paton recognizes fully, and must be overcome. But they are
not the most important. The crucial matter is deeper. It involves the things in the world which divide man from man,
and in so doing eat their way into the church, separating
Christian from Christian.

Too frequently, Christians have not realized that this has
happened. A sentimental feeling that the rude and rugged
world is somehow shut out of the church has made Christians
blind leaders of the blind. But the world is very much in the
church, with its cruelty, its hardness, its callous lack of love.
To realize what this means for the foundations of unity among
the faithful is one of the first and most important steps in the
growth of that unity. Until every congregation knows how
much of the world's divisions it reflects, and how these divisions
cut the nerve of its own unity, there will be no unity in Christ
worthy of the name.

Two great divisions tear the modern world and the church
within it. The first of these is race. Over this question, man is
divided from man, and Christian from Christian. White and
colored are two separate groups, by law in South Africa, by
law or custom in the United States, by the force of historical
treatment in the Far East and Central Africa. The churches
have nowhere fully bridged the gap. Following the pattern of
their surrounding culture, animated by the fears of the general
society, bound by the prejudice of their color, they have kept
the colored and the white apart in the Body of Christ. In such
a final way have they acquiesced to the general injustice. The
result is a separation of the spirit which is as deep as physical
segregation is extensive. No amount of theological agreement
among the denominations can overcome this deep disunity.
What meaning does agreement covering Baptist principles have

in southern United States? This separation cuts across matters of the faith and makes a mockery of any purely theological and ecclesiastical agreement. It is this spiritual separation which is the most damaging, although it is inextricably interlocked with segregation. Here, prejudice on the one side and bitterness on the other set the one against the other so that the gospel of reconciliation is empty and without meaning. The church is at the same time the victim and the cause of a division which strikes at the deepest reaches of men's lives.

A second division involves a whole galaxy of factors. It is the division between the East in the sense of Russia and the West in the sense of the United States. We need not here analyze the philosophic, economic, political, cultural, and military factors involved in this conflict. We must emphasize its effect upon the unity of the church. Men on the one side are gathered up in an outlook and in a conception of their Christian faith which has hardly any point of contact with the conceptions of men on the other side of this conflict. Christian words cease to mean the same thing. Trust is infected with suspicion. Even the contact of letters, visits, and meetings is barred, and if attempted, is regarded by both sides with suspicion. What is the attitude of Christians on the one side of this conflict to be toward those on the other? Is each to write the others off, rule them out of the church? It is easy for us to ask, shaking our heads and clucking our tongues, whether they will let the claims of the People's Democracies come before the claims of Christ. But for us the question is whether we shall let the claims of democratic capitalism stand above the claims of Christ. Upon the answer to this question will depend the unity of the church at one of its most crucial points.

The way in which the church meets these two divisions will indeed test the strength of her unity. Behind them both is the movement of vast bodies of people, people strongly on the march and people strongly on the defensive. Emotions run higher in reference to these two matters than in reference to anything else. Truth becomes distorted here more tragically than in any other areas of life. In reference to race, the church has shown itself weaker than most institutions; it is hard fact that greater progress has been made in educational, governmental, and economic institutions than in the churches. In reference to the East-West problem, the church, though it has been able to do pitifully little, has shown itself stronger than most institutions. In either case, the battle is now in progress.

III

How can we conclude? From one viewpoint it looks as though our agreements in the faith amounted to nothing; they are all but destroyed by underlying disagreements which in fact amount to a conflict of completely different views of the faith. From quite a different perspective, theological agreement, even if it were achieved, still must stand the acid test, in the face of little achievement so far, of bridging the great divisions which curse humanity and the church today.

The key is found in the fact that we should not take our present theological agreements as principles, but rather as living convictions, seriously meant. The details of that statement about God, Christ, man, and the church are not important. What is important is what they represent. Put another way, they are the statement of the fact that we are held in the grip of a common reality, which is God in Christ, a reality which will not let us go, perverse and foolish oft though we stray. Even if at times we do not see how it is possible, we are kept together by God. This is the true meaning of the formation of the World Council of Churches. Popular opinion looked for another Pentecost at Amsterdam and in disappointment that it did not appear, failed to see the real work which the Holy Spirit did there. At the same moment when our deepest difference was dimly seen, the churches agreed to stay together.

It is within this reality, or rather under the guidance of this reality, that we must continue to work on all fronts. For neither the unity of man with man, nor of Christian with Christian, is made by human hands. The whole course of history is testimony to that. Unity comes because the sovereign will of God prevails over our perverseness. He creates unity, among men and within the church.

CHAPTER FOUR

❧

Unity on the World Scale

THE GROWTH OF UNITY on the world scale, to borrow words of W. A. Visser 't Hooft, "reminds one of the development of a theme in a symphony. At first one or two instruments introduce the new melody and one expects that the other instruments will take it up. But no, the theme disappears in the mass of sound. Here and there it tries to disengage itself, but its time is not yet. Suddenly it comes out clearly and dominates all other sounds."

In 1952, the focal point of Christian unity on the world scale is the World Council of Churches. Over forty years of background are involved, however, in this present situation. Those forty years have seen a mass of movements, influences, and interests weaving in and out among one another and gradually working into one another. The following list, which will be the subjects of the succeeding paragraphs, will help to indicate what varied factors have been involved:

Different concerns about the mission of the church in the world
Distinct but overlapping theological concerns
The influence of lay conviction and work, both adult and youth

 Consolidation among the churches themselves
 The reaction of the churches to World War II

At each of these points Christians in the churches have seemed
to come to life. Our starting point is the year 1910, the year of
the great world Christian missionary conference; and during
the following period, widespread activity under these general
headings has been characteristic of Christians around the world.
The result has been the emergence of an increasing harmony in
the general movement toward unity, and with this harmony, a
developing power.

I

The historical point of departure is two different interests
appearing within a general concern for the mission of the
church in the world.

 The first of these is the vision of unity within the foreign
missionary enterprise. The awakening of missionary interest in
the United States in the latter part of the nineteenth century
and early twentieth century was not isolated. It was accompanied by a similar renewal of conviction in Great Britain,
and a definite but less extensive interest among the churches of
the continent of Europe. As a result, missionaries went forth
in great numbers to the islands of the sea, to Asia, to Africa.
Their work bore fruit, but they discovered quickly that alone
and separated from each other they were weak. Moreover, it
became evident that as people in those lands began to understand and accept the gospel, they could make little sense of the
ecclesiastical and theological differences which had appeared
in western Christianity. Serious consideration of unity was
demanded. The first notable and world-wide occasion for it
was the Edinburgh Conference on the World Mission of the

Church in 1910. Extremely careful preparation, representative participation, and leadership which was both wise and courageous made the Edinburgh Conference of permanent importance. It desired to perpetuate its influence, and did so by two means. One was the establishment of a Continuation Committee to push forward the interests of the Conference as a whole. The other was by the formation, under the Continuation Committee, of regional and national councils, which in due course became a series of some thirty-two National Christian Councils in thirty-three different lands. In 1922, work having been interrupted by World War I, these now developed National Christian Councils were brought together by the Continuation Committee into a permanent structure. The International Missionary Council was formed, composed of representatives of the national councils. It exists today as one of the chief ecumenical agencies. It is not a council of churches. It is composed of representatives of missionary societies in the lands of the "older" or "sending" churches, and of councils in the lands of the "younger" churches, the latter being made up of the young churches, missions, and other Christian agencies in these lands. Since its founding in 1922, the International Missionary Council has held two large world gatherings, one at Jerusalem in 1928 and the other in Madras, India, in 1938. Both were of great importance in the gathering movement toward unity, in addition to their significance, of course, for the task of world evangelism. They registered the fact indelibly that the missionary task brings with it, as a simultaneous reflex, the conviction that unity is necessary.

A second interest within the total mission of the church to the world likewise added drive to the movement toward unity. Christians in the United States, Britain and to a lesser degree on the Continent, had become aware not only of their missionary responsibility but also of their responsibility for society. In particular, concern for world peace pressed upon the Christian conscience. In 1914, upon American initiative, and influenced in part by the unity developing in the missionary enterprise, a group of individuals formed the World Alliance for International Friendship Through the Churches. Its work for international peace illustrates a growing concern over the relation of Christian faith to social problems. Its method demonstrates a demand for unity. In its well-attended and representative meetings, occurring regularly, as well as in its work of collaboration among Christians from different countries and different churches, it brought together many who gained both vision and experience in the development of Christian unity.

This interest in social questions broadened. A movement was formed to consider the whole range of problems involved in the life and work of the churches in relation to society. Gathered dramatically at a world conference at Stockholm, Sweden, in 1925—a meeting which has come to be regarded as one of the key points in the succession of world ecumenical meetings —Christians from the Continent and Britain and North America saw again the need for unity. The great issues for society could not be faced, much less solved, in isolation. The committee appointed to carry on after the Conference was charged in the first instance "to perpetuate and strengthen the spirit of fellowship which this Conference so happily exemplifies." In 1930, the committee became the Universal Christian Council for Life and Work, carrying on a substantial program of contact with individual Christians and churches, and of study and research. Undoubtedly the most impressive achievement of the Life and Work Movement was the preparation and holding of the Oxford Conference on Church, Community, and State in 1937. What had begun tentatively and under a cloud of skep-

ticism and criticism in 1925, had now reached the stature of a
great event toward which Christians in Europe, Asia, and
America looked with hope and expectation. In part, this was
due to the change in the world scene: a world-wide depression,
the Nazi menace, and the awesome approach of war made the
subject matter of this conference of crucial importance.
Churches did not need to be argued into the conviction that in
unity there is strength; the threat of opposing forces made that
lesson all too clear. As we shall note later on, the time was ripe
for the churches to consider the formation of a comprehensive
and permanent structure for co-operation and unity. Between
1910 and 1937, the drive of Christians toward world evangelism and the desire of the churches to grapple with the great
problems of society had alike produced a demand for unity
that was not to be gainsaid.

II

Developing simultaneously, and in part involved in the movement we have just described, was a concern that the churches
face certain theological issues together. This need was felt in
the Life and Work Movement. For some time it operated under
the superficial slogan "Doctrine divides, but service unites."
The Stockholm Conference had not adjourned, however, without the recognition on the part of at least some that fundamental theological questions were involved in the question of
the church's function in society. What, for instance, is the
meaning of the Kingdom of God for the social task of the
church, and what is the relation of the church itself to
the Kingdom of God? How should the church be related to the
state—as servant? as equal? as critic? as supreme over the
state? On what basis and in what terms may the church be any

of these? Again, what is the relationship of the evangelistic
function of the church to its task in achieving social justice?
In short, what is the function of the church in society? Problems were raised which at once struck into the very heart of
Christian theology; and they so forced themselves upon those
responsible for the movement that the Oxford Conference became in truth as much a conference dealing with theology as
it was a conference dealing with social problems. This meant,
of course, that the inherent reaction from a social concern to
a concern for theology carried with it a further impetus in the
development of unity. The theological questions could not be
answered on behalf of the whole church without being considered among all the churches. And once any of the theological issues which underlie the problem of the church in society
had been raised, there had automatically been raised also the
problem of the unity of the church.

During the same time period, the question of the unity of
the church, in its deepest theological aspects, was being faced
in full measure. A single delegate at the World Missionary
Conference at Edinburgh in 1910, Bishop Charles Brent of the
Protestant Episcopal Church in the United States, became convinced at that conference of the pressing need to consider
questions of church unity directly. It was not enough, to his
tough-minded outlook, to try to co-operate in the work of the
church without at the same time dealing with the deepest problems of the church's unity. Persuading his own church to take
up the cause, he was instrumental in the convening at Lausanne, Switzerland, in 1927, of a world conference on Faith
and Order. This conference had been preceded by a vast cor-
respondence among church leaders and a number of smaller
meetings, but it was the event of importance. It differed from
the missionary conference of 1910 and the life and work con-

ference of 1925 not only in subject matter but in method and composition. It was convened not only to search out unity but to raise problems and find disagreements, not of course for the sport involved but that the unity might be more realistic. To do this in the most responsible fashion, it sought representatives who were accredited delegates from their churches and thus came in an official capacity. It has been characteristic of the Faith and Order Movement as a whole that an honest facing of differences, and a sense of close responsibility to the churches, have dominated its method. The Lausanne conference issued a common message to the world which is one of the classic statements of the Christian faith. Its authority still rings true, and it forms much of the basic theological agreement which exists among the churches. Beyond this, its attention was directed principally to the doctrine of the church.

The Lausanne Conference followed the now established procedure. A Continuation Committee was created, charged with the work of continued consultation and with the calling of another world conference in due course. This second meeting was held in Edinburgh, in 1937, immediately following the Oxford Conference of the Life and Work Movement. The objective was the same: to discover both unity and difference. The significant discovery of the Edinburgh Conference was that no obstacle to unity existed in the whole range of the church's theology, save in reference to the doctrine of the church. As we have noted, however, the Conference in its report somewhat uneasily recorded its suspicion that behind the whole matter lay two widely different total concepts of the church, which in fact would color agreements as well as define disagreements in a different context. It may, however, with good reason be argued that the effect of both the Lausanne and Edinburgh conferences has far outstripped the specific findings of either. The

movement toward unity was mightily put forward by the sheer
fact that in facing the deepest differences they could find, the
churches did not shrink away from each other into further isolation, but repeatedly reaffirmed their determination to remain
in fellowship with each other, searching actively for an answer
to the great and humiliating problems of difference among
them. A single-minded concern with problems of theology had
led to the same point as had the movements for world evangelism and for the social responsibility of the churches.

III

Another set of influences was operating at the same time. One
of the earliest forces on the scene was the laymen's and laywomen's movements associated in the Young Men's Christian
Association and Young Women's Christian Association and
student Christian movements. The role of the Y.M.C.A and
Y.W.C.A., each one gathered together under a World's Committee—as early as 1855 for the Y.M.C.A.—was indirect but
important. Particularly in the earlier days of their life, both
movements, but especially the Y.M.C.A., were conscious of a
very close relationship to the churches and of a definite evangelistic responsibility and function. In the United States, the
specifically religious purpose of the lay movements tended to
diminish. Yet, in the main, the vision of laymen throughout the
world was kindled in the young men and young women as they
worked together, irrespective of church affiliation, for common
Christian purposes. In the lands of the younger churches particularly, their role in evangelism and the achievement of unity
was marked. They provided a background of lay support and
interest in the more churchly developments that has ever been
a strength. Moreover, they contributed leadership which has

played a large part in the general ecumenical development.

It is, however, to the student Christian movements, in which the Y.M.C.A. and Y.W.C.A. had a large part, that tribute must be paid for aggressive and radical ecumenical pioneering. Existing in the different countries of Europe, Britain, the United States, and the Far East, and joined together in the World's Student Christian Federation since 1895, the student Christian movements met together on a world basis, and kept in contact with each other through their speakers and their literature. Not a part of the churches officially, the student Christian movements and the Federation have regarded themselves in both a spiritual and a functional sense as close to the churches, indeed as the representatives of the church on the university campuses of the world. Free from ecclesiastical control, with the imagination stimulated by the intellectual climate of the great universities and the small colleges as well, they have been able to point the way not only in matters of unity but also in the world mission of the church. Were not the Student Volunteers the backbone of the missionary enterprise at its height? It was, as we mentioned, among students that world Christian unity became a fact very early in the process. And it is from the student movements that some of the greatest of ecumenical leadership has come, and continues to come. In the student movements, conviction, training, and vision have been molded into a veritable spearhead for the ecumenical movement as a whole.

Student interest developed into a general youth movement, on the whole but not exclusively a layman's development. Two dramatic events have crystallized the ecumenical movement among youth and provided also a great source of strength for it. The World Conference of Christian Youth, held at Amsterdam in 1939, met four weeks before the outbreak of war. It was not primarily a conference for the production of findings. It was a conference where Christian young people from all over the world and out of the many churches of the world met their Lord together. *Christus Victor,* the theme of the Conference, was more than a mere theme. It stood for a reality that gripped the hearts of those gathered in Amsterdam. They were all people who went back into the armies and into the resistance movements and into the struggling churches. Yet, as person after person testified, out of prison camps, out of concentration camps, out of the refugee universities of China, out of the armies, reality never left them. It was the substance of hope for them in the dark and terrible years. Christian unity among the youth leaders of the churches had come alive because it had been grounded in a knowledge of the presence of the Lord. The first to gather together after the war was over were the youth of the churches. They met in Oslo, still bearing the signs of the horrible war, in 1947, returning from the armies and from the resistance and the struggles and the hardships, from fear and pain and the realms of death. "Jesus Christ is Lord." They marched through the streets of the war-weary city of Oslo with that banner on their shoulders. It bore testimony to what they believed in spite of what they and the world had been through. The situation, of course, had shifted and changed. Postwar problems were to the fore. Asian nationalism was rising. Tension was keen. Yet as at Amsterdam before the war, the unity of Christ the Lord was real. From that Oslo meeting there came a knowledge of that fact, which still has its power in the wider ecumenical movement.

In addition to these movements among laymen, the postwar period has seen additional revival of lay power and initiative in the church. New lay movements have sprung up. Their contribution has perhaps been an indirect one; for their chief

concern has been with the continued vitality of the church and
the power of its impact upon the life of the nations. They have
arisen principally in Europe, and in general are the result of
the revival of church life and power which took place during
the war. Then it was borne in upon clergy and laymen alike
that the church is in truth the whole people of God, that the
layman in his life in the world indeed in a sense *is* the church.
Moreover, it has been made clear that the gospel is to be
preached, particularly in this modern world, most effectively
by laymen to laymen at work in the world. Here the gospel can
be spoken with authority, in terms relevant to the life of men
at work. In Germany, in Holland, in Scandinavia, and in
Greece, notably, such laymen's movements have spontaneously
appeared. The World Council of Churches established the
Ecumenical Institute chiefly in order to bring these various
groups into contact with each other. All give evidence of a
deep concern for the unity of the church, as well as for the renewal of its life. They have formed a powerful background for
advance in the cause of Christian unity in these years since the
war.

IV

Another motif in the symphony has not resulted in the development of a comprehensive world theme, but has rather been
heard here and there throughout the churches of the world.
Between 1910 and 1948 an accelerated consolidation has taken
place among the churches themselves, which, though not resulting directly in a world organization, has been of substantial importance in the development of the general movement of unity.

There has been, especially if one compares this with previous periods, an outburst of unions among the churches. They

have not been the result of any concerted push; they have been spontaneous. Nor have they been confined to one confession or even one family of churches, still less to one area of the world. Although we cannot enter into the details of these unions, even to the point of mentioning the names of the 144 churches involved, it will give us an idea of the range and extent of unions to indicate something of their general categories. The bare list runs as follows:

Organic unions within confessions or families of churches:
> 26 unions in U.S.A., Scotland, England, France, Holland, Switzerland, Italy, Central Africa, Gold Coast, West Africa, South Africa, Madagascar, India, China, Korea, Mexico, Brazil, involving 66 previously existing churches.

Organic unions across confessional lines:
> 14 unions in U.S.A., Canada, Rhodesia, India, Siam, China, Japan, Philippines, Guatemala, Puerto Rico, involving 43 previously existing churches.

Federal unions, not complete organic unions:
> 3 unions in Switzerland, Spain, and Germany, involving 33 churches.

Negotiations for intercommunion completed in various forms:
> 6 affecting churches in U.S.A., England, Sweden, Finland, India, and the Philippines, involving 9 churches.

Negotiations for organic union still in progress:
> 16 in U.S.A., South Africa, Nigeria, Madagascar, Iran, India, Pakistan, Ceylon, Australia, Formosa, involving 59 churches.

Negotiations for closer fellowship short of organic union, still in progress:
> 7 in Canada, Great Britain, Ireland, and Australia, involving 18 churches.

It is important to note the types of churches, at least by families, which have been involved in this consolidation:

Organic unions within confessions or families of churches:
> Anglican, Baptist, Lutheran, Presbyterian, Methodist, Reformed, Congregationalist, Evangelical. It must be noted that not all of the churches of these families have suddenly united; but rather that some churches within each of these families have united.

Organic unions across confessional lines:
> Presbyterian, Baptist, Methodist, Congregationalist, Reformed, Anglican, Evangelical, United Brethren, Christian, and some United Churches. It must be noted that not all of these churches have united with each other; nor must one draw conclusions from this list as to which have united with each other. It is meant to indicate here that churches within these families have united with churches across confessional lines.

Federal unions, not complete organic unions:
> Reformed, Methodist, Evangelical, Lutheran. (The same note applies here as above.)

Negotiations for intercommunion completed in various forms:
> Anglican, Lutheran, Old Catholic, Mar Thoma Syrian, Polish National Catholic, Philippine Independent. (Above note applies here.)

Negotiations for organic union still in progress:
> Congregational, Methodist, Presbyterian, Anglican, Baptist, Lutheran, Disciples, Evangelical and Reformed, Society of Friends, and some United Churches. Note that this category includes both organic unions within confessional lines and across confessional lines. (The same note as above applies here also.)

Negotiations for closer fellowship short of organic union:
Anglican, Congregational, Methodist, Presbyterian, United Church of Canada. (Above note applies here.)

Note: For detailed information on all negotiations still in progress, see Stephen Neill, *Towards Church Union 1937-1952, Faith and Order Commission Papers,* No. 11.

A second form of consolidation among the churches has been the formation of national councils of churches. We have already indicated the formation of the council in the United States. Others exist in virtually every country where there is a significant variety of denominations: in Great Britain and the countries of the British Commonwealth and in the lands of the younger churches. There is no council of churches for Europe, but in Switzerland and Germany the federal unions mentioned above serve virtually as such, and in Holland an "ecumenical council" has been organized. These councils are very uneven in their strength, varying from the imposing structure of the National Council of the Churches of Christ in the U.S.A. to those which consist virtually of an annual meeting and the work of a single paid employee. Yet they all represent a commitment of the churches of their respective territories to work together and to consult with one another, and as such they have contributed to the general consolidation which has taken place among the churches themselves.

The third form of unity among the churches has been of a quite different order. This, akin to the organic unions which have taken place within confessional lines, has been the development of world associations of churches within confessional groupings. The Baptists, Disciples, Congregationalists, Friends, Methodists, Presbyterians, Lutherans, and Anglicans have all formed world confessional agencies. Some of them are

strong and well organized, carrying on extensive programs, as
the Lutheran World Federation. Others are but infrequent
meetings for purposes of consultation, as the Friends. The
Anglican body, the Lambeth Conference, one of the first, carries a very great prestige but has no continuing organization.
No single pattern obtains which can describe them all. Arising
in relatively recent times, they have been characterized as a confessional reaction to the general development of the ecumenical
movement. A more charitable statement of the matter would be
that they represent the outreach of like-minded people to each
other, and some have explicitly stated that their purpose is to
develop a particular contribution to the ecumenical movement
itself. The discussion concerning the value and disvalue of the
confessional agencies is likely to be charged with some emo-
tion. It cannot be doubted that within their particular frame of
reference they have contributed to an understanding across national and cultural divisions, and that they have contributed a
heightened sense of the worth of their respective traditions to
the general movement toward unity, thus enriching the whole.
If some present tendencies were to be strongly developed,
these agencies could damage Christian unity as it has so far
developed; there are fortunately but few signs that either will
happen.

V

The reaction of the churches to World War II, unexpectedly
enough, contributed in large measure to unity among them.
The root of the struggle, in country after country, was for the
church to be the church. The pressure, in whatever terms and
with whatever force it was exerted, was for the church to become something other than the Body of Christ. In Europe, the
Nazi government sought to make of the church an agent of its

alien ideology. In Britain and America, popular opinion, although not the government, sought to make the church merely the buttress of the national defense. Throughtout, it had to struggle to maintain its own integrity. Fortunately, it had learned both a negative and a positive lesson. In World War I, the churches in all countries had acquiesced too readily to these same types of pressures and, in the years immediately following, the price which had to be paid was high. Endless discussions indicated that fellowship had been shattered and could only painfully be renewed. This lesson had been clear; it must not happen again. On the positive side, the growth of the ecumenical movement, and in particular the far-reaching influence of the Oxford Conference in which this problem had been foreseen and dealt with, proved their great value. Leaders of the churches, and to some extent the churches themselves, had experienced a deep and true unity, too precious to let go.

Beyond this, the churches themselves showed a truly wonderful resilience, a capacity to resist the pressure, and ability to transcend it. In Europe, this took the form of the Christian resistance which, led in large part by those who had participated in the ecumenical movement, kept a clear-sighted hold on the true faith and nature of the church, often paying the price of torture and death. They did not yield to the false ideas of the Nazi conquerors; and by asserting their independence, by keeping in touch through the underground press and the illegal couriers with the outside world and with each other, they kept the integrity and unity of the faith. There are few more heroic stories in the history of the church than those of the Christian resistance in the war.

In Britain and America the response was of course different. There the Christians turned their attention to ministering to needs caused by war, and in great measure to the problems of postwar reconstruction. Some of the clearest thinking in reference to this intricate issue was done by Christian groups in Britain and America alike, and their influence with government and in the United Nations has not been wanting. As the war drew to a close, attention, especially in prosperous America, was turned to the problem of relief and reconstruction, a response of mercy which grew in volume and was not confined to the victors, but was given in generous measure to the vanquished as well.

Two events at the end of the war dramatize the ability of the church to keep its integrity and its unity.* During a broadcast in Japan, which was monitored in the United States, a Christian government administrator referred to a meeting held in 1941 in California between Japanese and United States church leaders. This was the cue for a move to be made by the American churches at the end of the war. They sent a deputation to the enemy country, a deputation which was able to meet with Japanese Christians, and on the one hand be convinced of the integrity of those of the former enemy country, and on the other hand convince them of the desire of the United States churches for reconciliation. In October of 1945, a delegation of American, British, Dutch, French, and Swiss churchmen went to Stuttgart, Germany, to meet with German church leaders. They were greeted with a full recognition of the guilt of the German nation and of the implication of the German churches in that guilt. They could assure their German brethren of their desire for reconciliation. Hardly had the guns ceased firing than the unity which had existed in fact throughout the war was again visible. It was undoubtedly a different and a deeper unity than anything that had been known before. The

---

* A third, less noticed, was a meeting at the close of hostilities, between American and Italian Protestants.

suffering out of which it was born had been responsible for that. Yet it was part and parcel of what had begun to be forged in the years of ecumenical work prior to the war; for it was all a gift of the Lord of the church.

Specific projects, some of vast scope, were carried on during and after the war, which both demonstrated and added to the unity of the churches. One of these was the work known as Orphaned Missions, a most remarkable demonstration of truly ecumenical spirit. The missions in the Far East and Africa which had been supported by the missionary societies of the Continent were cut off from their sources of support as a result of the war. Through the International Missionary Council, which co-ordinated the effort throughout the whole period, support for them was found from different churches and nations, so that no missionary at all during the war had to cease his work for lack of support. Again, there was a united ministry to the great mass of war prisoners, carried on by the Y.M.C.A. and by the World Council of Churches, which was then operating—as we shall soon see—under its Provisional Committee. Through this service, which was supported by Christians of all churches, the men in the prison camps were given help for their spiritual life, so important in maintaining hope and purpose among them, as well as books and recreational material to help keep them occupied through the dark and idle days. Third, information was provided by the world agencies located in Geneva, principally by the World Council. Its headquarters in that thriving city, the center of so much during the war, maintained contact across all the battle lines, and could in one form or another pass on information around the world concerning the state of the churches and of their leaders. This was one of the largest services which contributed to the main-

tenance of unity during the war; by virtue of it, isolation was
not allowed to creep in.

The great problem of refugees, that still monstrous human
problem, also commanded the attention of the churches, and
was—to the limit of ability and of funds available—met
through co-operative action, again through the World Council
of Churches. Many were saved from almost certain death by
assisting them to escape; other thousands were helped in their
miserable life in the great camps. This work still continues,
and grows even greater; one of the most moving acts of the
churches in common has been their constant, generous, and
helpful work in behalf of the refugees of Europe and Asia.
Finally, toward the close of the war, the work of reconstruction and interchurch aid and material relief loomed as virtually
the major work of the World Council, and certainly the most
vivid instance of the working unity of the church. Tens of millions of dollars were given and spent in helping people and
churches stricken by the war. Funds came from countries outside of Europe, principally America, and were given to
churches and Christians in Europe purely on the basis of need.
Former political alliances did not shape that giving, neither
did denominational affiliation determine it. The result has been
that testimony after testimony has indicated that through the
mutual helpfulness of the churches which were still prosperous
to those who had had everything taken from them, the greatest
unity of all had been made unmistakably vivid: *By this shall
all men know that ye are my disciples, if ye have love one to
another.*

VI

The newest of the ecumenical agencies is the World Council of Churches. In the course of this chapter we have already mentioned others which have been formed in the past period and have tried to indicate something of their basic function. The World's Alliance of the Y.M.C.A.'s, founded as far back as 1855, was the first. The World's Student Christian Federation and the World's Young Women's Christian Association are both of long history. Another, which we have not had occasion to mention hitherto, is the World Council of Christian Education, concerned to provide contact among the religious education agencies of the churches throughout the world, growing originally out of the world Sunday School movement.

From the viewpoint of the unity of the churches, almost unquestionably the most important of these agencies founded during the last forty years is the International Missionary Council. It is the agency through which the great majority of the Christians in the lands of the younger churches have ecumenical contact with the Christians of the West. Through its great world meetings and its consultative processes between meetings, the International Missionary Council has kept before the churches, which so frequently forget it, their all important responsibility for world evangelism. As we have seen, it is in the nature of the case impossible to do this without also providing an impetus for unity among the churches. This is the more true since the younger churches frequently see the demand for unity with more clarity and urgency than we do in the West, and their participation in the ecumenical movement through the work of the International Missionary Council has resulted in an important contribution to the churches of the West at this point.

In one sense the total movement toward unity, starting feebly in the early days, gathering strength at first gradually and then rapidly, forms the background out of which the World Council of Churches has been created. It is important, however, to understand clearly the sense in which this is true. It cannot be justifiably said that this great movement of unity, appearing in so many forms and places, is the background for the creation of a specific organization, even if that organization may be called a World Council of Churches. The structure of this organization, its committees, staff, budget, and its policies and programs are all too weak and partial for any such claim to be made; indeed, such a claim should not be made of even a strong organization. In a way, the organization called the World Council of Churches is unimportant. The thing which is of very deep importance, and the thing for which all of the foregoing movement toward unity is properly a background, is the will among the churches—at present expressed in the World Council of Churches—to join with each other and to stay together. The way in which that will is expressed may, and one hopes in due course will, change. But the growth of the determination, and the actions whereby that determination becomes a very tangible thing, must deepen and become even more pronounced.

The history of the formation of the World Council of Churches should be read in this light, in the light, that is, of the growth within the churches of a will to join together in the common pursuit of the work of Christ in the world and in the common pursuit of the unity of Christ in that work. Unquestionably the idea of a *world* council grew out of the missionary movement and out of the growing unity of the missionary enterprises around the world. There was a time, for instance at the Stockholm Conference of Life and Work in 1925, when the younger churches were represented in the most inadequate way. That was not a world movement. The impression made, however, first by the growth and vigor of these younger churches themselves, and by the great world conferences of Jerusalem in 1928 and Madras in 1938, at which the younger churches were present in force and refreshing vitality, made it clear that any really comprehensive ecumenical agency must in truth be a world agency.

The conviction that the World Council must be a council of *churches* cannot be so precisely located. In part, it grew out of the stirrings among the churches themselves, stirrings felt in unions and in the development of national councils of churches. Work with other churches close at home made it possible to envisage work among all the churches on a world scale. In part, the realization came through both the policy and the work of the Faith and Order Movement. Its policy was always one of adhering very closely to the churches; its conferences were made up of persons officially representing their churches; the findings of the conferences were systematically referred to the churches for their comment. Its work revealed that the very center of unity must be found, as in the contemporary situation it is denied, at the very heart of the churches. Unity involved in associations of individuals not closely related to the churches sidesteps the central point. Beyond this, the developing work of the Life and Work Movement pointed to the necessity of a closer relation to the churches. The problem for that movement was the problem of the church in relation to society. Moreover, the pressure of world events, culminating in World War II, made it increasingly evident that informal alliances could not provide the answer. If there was to be strength of response to the pagan threats, to the disaster of war, it must be a response coming from the heart of the church. From every viewpoint it became clear that the next step in ecumenical action was the formation of a council which on the one hand would be a world council, and on the other a council of the churches themselves.

The concrete proposals were made and the initiative was taken by the two movements known as Faith and Order and Life and Work. They were the two ecumenical movements on the scene which were the most closely related to the churches. The third major agency, the International Missionary Council, it will be remembered, was not related to the churches as such, but rather to national councils which, in turn, were made up of the missionary societies of the churches. In all of the developments which led to the creation of the World Council of Churches, close collaboration was maintained with the International Missionary Council, but it was not one of the founding agencies. A series of proposals by individuals, among whom the late Archbishop of Canterbury, William Temple, was perhaps the chief, and a series of small meetings, among which that at Westfield College, London, in July, 1937, was the most important, resulted in a plan for a world council of churches, to be a "body representative of the churches and caring for the interests of Life and Work and Faith and Order respectively." World Conferences on Life and Work and on Faith and Order had been organized to convene later that same summer; the proposal was put before each conference and adopted virtually unanimously.

Three more stages were required, however, before the Council could become definitely established. First, it was necessary to develop a constitution, and it was necessary that the churches themselves be consulted about the character of that constitution. Accordingly, a conference of representatives of the churches was convened a year later at Utrecht (1938) and a provisional constitution adopted. The Committee appointed jointly by the Oxford and Edinburgh Conferences, called the Committee of Fourteen, became a Provisional Committee and functioned under the constitution provisionally adopted at Utrecht. It was thought that it would function for only three years and that it would be responsible chiefly for calling a large Assembly.

The Provisional Committee was forced to function for ten years. War broke out in 1939 and all hopes were deferred. More than that, heavy responsibility descended upon the Provisional Committee of the World Council of Churches and its slender structure, headed by W. A. Visser 't Hooft as General Secretary. The war work and projects which we have indicated above were carried out by this group. The growing unity of the churches themselves during the tragedy of the war and the exceedingly wise and courageous leadership of the World Council made the cause prosper during these ten formative years. This was the deep spiritual factor of these years: that unity was forged deeper than it had been before. The legal process of this period, and the second remaining step in the formation of the World Council of Churches structure, was the submission of the provisional constitution to the churches. By 1946, ninety-three churches had voted to join the World Council on the basis of the constitution, and by 1948, one hundred and forty-eight churches had voted to join. The fundamental basis for membership in the World Council is an expression on the part of the churches of their faith in Christ: any church may be a member which "accepts Jesus Christ as God and Saviour."

The third and final remaining step involved the convening of a World Assembly of the churches, which was held in Amsterdam in 1948. It was a deeply moving meeting, for with extreme simplicity a motion was put, adopted, and commemorated with brief silent and spoken prayer to constitute a World Council of Churches. Therein was the movement of the Holy Spirit at Amsterdam. It was not a sudden movement. The preparation for it had been long. But it was a tangible movement and it resulted in a definite act. Henceforth, the churches themselves were in a close and permanent association, an association carrying implications for the life of the churches which are only beginning to be explored.

CHAPTER FIVE

❦

Next Steps

IT IS INEVITABLE that a discussion of the current movement toward unity in the churches should close with a statement of the "next steps." This movement is a dynamic thing, constantly developing. Put the other way around, it holds up an ideal which at once beckons to us and enters into us, urging us toward its fulfillment. It is in fact even more radically dynamic than that, for the unity of the church does not really consist of an ideal. We do not see an ideal of harmony and proportion to be attained, step by planned step. To speak of Christian unity is rather to speak of the kind of unity which exists among persons when they are bound together by love, the kind of love that makes one think of the other person first, his good and not one's own. The unity of the church is this love on the grand and profound scale. The unity of the church consists in the real presence of Christ in men's hearts, knitting them together. It is therefore a radical unity, striking deep and reaching wide. It is a dynamic unity, for it is made up of all the powerful elements of the human soul in touch with its Lord. Because this is the unity which holds us in its grip, the next step must always be a step of faith. We do not know precisely where

Christ will lead us; we trust only that he will lead us, and commit ourselves to follow. Yet because of the very fact that he works in us, in us who are in our present situation of unity and disunity in the church, it is likely that he will lead us along roads which branch out of this present situation. They may take unexpected turnings, as they have in the past, but the road in some sense is continuous.

At the close of the second chapter, we said that unity in the United States had taken a definite road. The same is largely true with the development of unity among the churches throughout the world. There have been a number of corporate unions, a few federal unions, a few agreements for intercommunion, but these have all been more the exception than the rule. The great avenue has been that of co-operation among churches. The question, therefore, of the next steps to be taken in achieving closer unity is whether this road should be wholly rebuilt or whether it should be strengthened and broadened. Is co-operation unsatisfactory, too short of the goal, and should it therefore be discarded as the means to unity or an expression of it? Or is it a legitimate direction to take, provided that it can be developed?

These questions really coalesce and become one problem. To raise the question of rebuilding the present road to unity is to force ourselves to recognize several related factors. We recognize that there is an ultimate Christian unity, just as there is an ultimate and perfect Christian moral life, the unity in Christ. We know, as soon as we dwell upon this deep and seamless unity, that none of the existing expressions of unity fulfill its character. Co-operation among those who will not unite with each other is not the fullness of unity in Christ. Organic union of institutions in which there is a mixture of the human and Christlike likewise falls short. All existing forms of unity therefore have before them both a guide and a judge—a guide which spurs them on to something closer and greater than they now have achieved; a judge which shows all too clearly their shortcomings. Whether as guide or as judge, the unity we must still attain is the unity of the Body of Christ. This in turn means that so far as the vision of Christ's unity has taken hold of us at all, we must live in a constant and acute tension. It is the tension between what He desires and what we have achieved. We are familiar enough with this tension in our moral living. In one sense, the problem of achieving greater unity is the problem of realizing the same tension in this area as we have realized in our moral life. For centuries, Christians have mouthed prayers concerning the One Church, feeling no sense of shame at living amid divisions. A great spiritual fact of the present era is that we are beginning to feel a sense of shame about our disunity, a knowledge that we sin by being divided from each other as surely as we sin in stealing and in murder. If we live in this tension, we shall live with open minds and spirits concerning all existing forms of Christian unity. We will not cling to co-operation or to organic union as being precious, because we will know that there is something more precious yet to be achieved. In this sense, we must count all as loss for Christ. And if this openness is not just a tunnel through which the wind blows, we will have with it an adventuresomeness, a drive to experiment, to create new forms of unity as we may be led to envisage them. Yet we will also have stability of outlook, not driven by every wind of doctrine but responsible to the main stream of God's leading toward his will, so far as we are given to understand it. To live in tension, thus, is not to live in a torn anguish. It is to live in such a way that the tension itself will pull us along. If we are to rebuild the road to Christian unity, therefore, we must bring all of these factors to bear upon the existing situation. God meets people where they are, and we are in the middle of the road of co-operation. The ultimate vision, and the tension between that vision and our present situation, must both be seen in relation to where we are now, and lived out in the midst of the contemporary scene.

Rebuilding thus becomes the task of strengthening and broadening the existing road. But this does not mean solidifying and entrenching the present structures of co-operation so that nothing new can come out of them. Rather, it means exploiting the commitments involved in present co-operation, deepening its spirit, challenging its presuppositions, bringing the whole under the guidance and the judgment of the unity of the Body of Christ. In this sense, the over-all task of the next steps is to strengthen and to broaden the existing highway.

I

As one thinks of what is involved in this process, certain assets and liabilities become evident which form the substance with which we must inevitably work.

The first asset is simply the fact that the ecumenical movement, now in 1952, is firmly established. We referred to the power of the conviction which upholds the structure of the National Council of Churches. Equally great conviction maintains the World Council of Churches, which, though much smaller in structure, involves its participating members in such profound struggles and against such overwhelming odds that only by the deepest faith can it be kept going. Unquestionably the ecumenical idea has taken root, with power. This carries with it immense implications. Just as you cannot have a tree without having wood, so you cannot have an ecumenical movement without at the same time having a vigorously dynamic situation. Such diverse elements are thrown together in the very fact of an ecumenical movement that the result is at once a situation of action and reaction and further action. For instance, at Amsterdam were gathered representatives from churches who lived in economies generally much more collectivistic than that of the U.S.A. The Christian interpretation of these economies was in the main positive and vigorous. They were also critical of the economy which lies at the basis of U.S. life. The reaction in the United States was immediate and pronounced. Out of this reaction has come continuing discussion. Again, Protestants, Anglicans, and Orthodox meet together. Unless they are to keep silent, they will be in tension with each other; for each word and sentence will have within it and behind it content and presuppositions which are either strange or unacceptable to the others. Minds will be in constant interaction. The ecumenical movement is like a team of wild horses: motion is assured, the problem being which direction it will take. When this is compounded with the turmoil of the world situation today, this frightful situation of fear and suspicion and persecution and homelessness, with the different perspectives and interests which it gives to Christians from the different countries, the depth and urgency of the inherent dynamics of the ecumenical situation become increased to a sometimes almost unbearable extent. Yet it is never wholly unbearable. It would be if there were only human desires behind the ecumenical movement. We would then be caught in an almost runaway situation, in which the only guide would be the force of the driver's hand. In saying, however, that the ecumenical movement has become established, we mean to say, at the deepest level, that the ecumenical vision has been really *seen*. The unity of the Body of Christ is not a mere phrase. It is something which has gripped people, and gripped them deeply. The inherent motion and the dynamic character of the ecumenical situation have an ultimate direction which is, we believe, assured. It will move because it cannot help it; it will move forward because God guides it. This is what is meant by saying that it is a movement of the Holy Spirit. This is our biggest asset.

A related asset is the widespread mood of self-criticism and the widespread vitality of Christians in country after country. One hears the demand that the church repent, until one is all but tired of it. One hears people castigating the church, analyzing its failure, laying bare its shame and its weakness, until there is virtually nothing more to be said on this score. There is danger here, the danger that we take self-criticism for true repentance, that we relieve our consciences simply by acknowledging how bad we are and doing nothing about it. Yet this mood of self-criticism is a powerful asset. *Nothing* could be done with churches which are self-righteous. The knowledge of weakness and failure is the beginning of repentance. In part, repentance has already taken place, and new life has appeared. The relatively new theological concern, arising in part in response to the challenge of science, in part in response to the political and military and economic disasters in the world, and in part in response to the insistent demand of God's Word, is evidence that the churches contain more than a sterile defensiveness. A sense of weakness and shame has in this area already turned into a positive search, new commitment, and the beginnings of fresh and vital proclamation of Christian truth. Similarly, there has been, for the most part in Europe but beginning also in the United States, a new conception of the vocation of the Christian layman, especially in regard to his work in the world. A dead movement would not thus reach out into the turmoil of the social scene; it would retreat into the ministrations of its appointed priestly officers. A deepened and more vigorous sense of lay discipleship, however, again— as it has so often in Christian history—establishes the basis for genuine renewal in the church. These are more than mere illustrations. The basis of Christian thought and the basis of the life of the Christian church are involved in these two positive reactions of the church to its position in the world. The mood of self-criticism is coupled with vitality of a new sort at crucial points in the life of the churches, to form a major asset in continued ecumenical advance.

II

Major liabilities appear, however, as one faces the possibility of further growth in Christian unity. First, there is the deterioration in the popular, and in some extent in the official, use of the word "ecumenical." Second, present ecumenical strategy and method is not sufficiently clear or bold to carry the weight of the required load. Third, the encroachment of the divisions of world society into the church divides it in a deep and terrible way. Fourth, we cannot define, much less surmount, just what our deepest difference is.

The word "ecumenical" has deteriorated; perhaps it never was rightly understood and properly used. It makes little difference which is true. The point is that we are in danger of losing our grip on the very concept of the thing we are after. Whether you come at it etymologically, or whether you approach it from the viewpoint of what is actually happening in the movement called ecumenical, the word involves a certain understanding of the mission of the church and the unity of the church, and of the relationship between the church's mission and its unity, and of the relationship of both of these to Christ the Lord. Christ is the Lord, and those who know in their depths what this means understand that it involves an impulse to move out of oneself into the realm of others. Love cannot be confined; it must envelop others within its circle. The church therefore which truly knows its Lord will move out into the circles which do not know him. The church which truly knows love will move into those areas of the world's life which do not understand its meaning or its reality. The way in which the church is thus impelled into the world is a matter of wide variation, involving different factors.* The central fact is that true knowledge of the Lord impels individuals as well as the Christian community into areas of life which do not know him. The same factor brings men into unity with one another. The love engendered by Christ has not only a propulsive quality, but it has a capacity to unite all those who in any fashion recognize and receive its power and reality. As Christ's love forces us into the world, it unites us with the fears and pain and hopes and achievements of the world, and it unites with us those in the world who come under its influence. It is therefore impossible to speak of unity as a mechanical thing for one to achieve while with the other hand, so to speak, one pursues a mission. We can speak rightly only of response to Christ the Lord, knowing that the inner quality of that response to him, which is caused by his response to us, involves simultaneously what we call mission and unity. This is what is involved in the correct use of the word "ecumenical." It has deteriorated to mean interdenominational, or world church, or the city council of churches, or the World Council of Churches.

---

* One of the most helpful treatments of this subject is *Christ and Culture*, by H. Richard Niebuhr, Harper & Brothers, New York, 1951.

It is not an organizational word. It is a spiritual word. It is a word which points to the true Christian community under its Lord.

This means that each Christian must give serious attention to his working concept of the church. We distinguish between a theoretical concept of the church and a working concept of it. Most persons who have any knowledge of the Bible or the creeds will define the church at once as the Body of Christ, the One, Holy, Catholic church. Most will also refer to the church as the congregation or the denomination. The difficulty is that the first definition, the one of the church as the Body of Christ, is for most people a verbal definition only, their working definition being of the church in terms of the congregation or denomination. It is this church that they work in and think of; it is this church that is the most real to them. To think of the church in ecumenical terms is in effect to make the biblical definition a working definition. The church is the Body of Christ, that *total* company of people who are brought together by the ties of Christ. So to believe is to think of the church as vastly more than an organization, vastly more than a place of worship, vastly more than an institution which ministers to "religious needs." It is to understand that the church is the community of those who are faithful to Christ, wherever they are, whatever they are doing, whether dispersed as they carry on their work and life in the world, whether gathered as they worship. Put in traditional language, the church is *wherever* the Word of God is preached and the sacraments administered. This preaching may be in word, or in deed, or in example. The sacrament will be the breaking of bread; but it will also be the constant sacrifice of our lives in devotion to Christ. The point is that neither preaching nor sacrament is confined: like the mustard seed, they expand. This is of course revolution for our churches. It turns them outward from their present institutional settings. It means that the church really is not to be found for the most part in these institutions, but it is found for the most part in the world where the faithful, though dispersed, are nevertheless united to Christ and to each other. This is of course not to advocate that congregations and denominations should be done away with. It is to say that a bigger concept can be worked into the warp and woof of Christian life than that by which most of us now live. Here is the place for every Christian to take hold, to work out in the midst of all the difficulties and joys of life. This is the very basis not only of the ecumenical movement but of the church's life itself. This is perhaps the major challenge of the ecumenical movement to the imagination, intelligence, and devotion of every Christian. It can be put in a simple and intensely personal question: How can I be a *true* member of the Body of Christ?

Principally because the ecumenical movement is new, it is hesitant and weak in its methods and strategy. Too frequently it has appeared that the agencies concerned with the ecumenical movement have stood on the outside of the churches, pleading for a hearing, delighted when in some small fashion it is granted. On every hand one hears the complaint that the ecumenical concept of the church is not living at the "grass roots." What is the real problem? It may be stated in some such fashion as this: that a concept of the church is being evolved in the ecumenical movement which is not the same as the concept which animates most of the denominations, and that the task is to modify the one by the other. The churches in general simply *have not had* a concept of unity which carried any power. Neither have the churches *as a whole* had a conspicuously driving concept of mission, irrespective of the work done by the missionary agencies. The result is the general weakness of the church which we now tragically feel on every hand. Our problem is to lodge a different concept of the church, namely, a truly ecumenical concept of the church, in each of the churches, with power. This does not imply a propaganda campaign to be launched on behalf of some idea that some interdenominational agency may dream up. It does imply the bringing of the churches under the Lord, together, that they may hear what he has to say.

We have hinted before at another way of stating the problem. Can the now well-developed road of co-operation stand the heavy-duty load of the official denominations? Many feel that it cannot, that the weight of the great, institutionalized churches will break the pioneering spirit, the freedom, the progress of ecumenical work as it has been known. A conservatism, they say, has already entered, a caution in all things which will increase and ultimately disintegrate the structure and the spirit of the unity that we have achieved. Although this is a danger, and a real one, it is our firm conviction that it is not an insuperable danger, but that it can be overcome. More than that, it is a problem which must be faced squarely, because in its solution lies the future of the movement toward unity. If one tries to avoid the issue, keeping the churches as such out of the ecumenical movement, which is to say keeping the ecumenical movement on the fringes of the churches, there is no important future ahead. It is among the *churches* that unity needs to be forged. Neither is there an important future in prospect if we yield to the danger, either by conscious and fearsome compromise with the forces that desire only a respectable status quo or by ignoring the problem and being led blindly by the forces of the status quo. We must meet the problem head on. In so doing, we face an urgent and intriguing issue. On the one hand, it is a sociological problem, the problem, namely, of changing institutions, which by their inherent logic as institutions resist change, without either alienating or destroying those institutions. This clearly is a matter which calls for the most astute sociological insight and understanding. On the other hand, it is a problem of Christian faith. Churches are never merely sociological phenomena. They are basically rooms in the total household of faith. Can the content, therefore, of the gospel be so conceived and lived within these institutions as to make them true to their basic character and genius? Can wisdom, freshness of approach, courage, and faith be so combined as to make this possible? These are the basic questions of ecumenical strategy. Until now, those engaged in the ecumenical movement have hardly begun to face them. In this sense, the present road of co-operation probably is not strong enough to stand the heavy-duty load of the official churches. Ecumenical strategy does not go deep enough, nor is it courageously enough advanced. But it can be reconceived, and remade in such a way as effectively to guide us further along the now clearly marked roadway.

In making suggestions, it must be clear that they are suggestions only. The real issue is for Christians who are committed to the ecumenical idea to tackle the problem themselves —with imagination, courage, and devotion. The suggestions may be of value or they may not. That is unimportant. The important thing is that Christian minds and energy be directed to the basic issue: How can the great ecumenical concept of the church be injected into existing Christian institutions and life with realism, with power, and with vision?

Hitherto, ecumenical strategy has been based upon the problem of getting a movement upward, as it were, and not directed toward getting a movement back downward. So far, we have

worked chiefly at getting representative opinion developed out
of the churches into an ecumenical gathering or organization,
there to be exhibited, publicized, discussed. We have been
largely content to leave the matter there. Yet this is not
enough. Wisdom cast to the winds frequently remains just that.
Attention must be given to getting ecumenically conceived
Christian truth back downward into the matrix of Christian
living. We offer four suggestions to this end:

First, ecumenical strategy should exploit the demands of the
external situation to the full. Some situations call for united
action by the churches and other Christian agencies, or no action at all. There can be, for instance, no approach to government within the nation or to the UN on a sectarian basis; it
must be a co-operative approach. We have come to take this
for granted, and to guide our actions accordingly. What, however, of other situations external to the church? Are there not
some, lacking the coercive power of government absolutely to
refuse a hearing except on their own terms, which nevertheless
do intrinsically demand ecumenical action? One thinks of
state universities, or universities and colleges as a whole for
that matter. Individualistic appeals to these campuses are permitted; but the best advice is that a co-operative voice is advis-
able if the evangelistic appeal is to be heard. Is this not an
external situation which in its nature demands ecumenical
planning, and which should therefore be pursued in this fashion? Exceedingly careful and honest inquiry will be needed to
discover which of the many situations external to the church
truly and intrinsically demand a co-operative approach, and
sloppy thinking on this subject will not advance the ecumenical
cause. Some situations may be more powerfully affected by a
sectarian approach. As ecumenical truth is gained on this sub-

ject, however, and as the demands of these external situations
are honestly met, a body of ecumenical habit will emerge.

Second, it is important to bring into ecumenical processes
those people who stand at the center of institutional life. Unless an institution is in the final stages of its development, so
rigid that only outright revolution may bring any change,
there is a real possibility of modification, even in fundamental
aspects of its life, provided that the modification is proposed
at the right time, in the right place, in reference to the right
need, and in the right terms. But who is qualified to judge these
matters save people who are at the heart of that institution?
In their constant search for new participants, ecumenical
agencies should proceed with due recognition of the strategic
role played by persons of responsibility. Such persons will be
able to translate the "ecumenical mind" into terms relevant to
their own institutions. The "ecumenical mind" thus enters into
the inner logic and working of the institution itself, rather than
standing on the outside appealing for a hearing. This is not to
argue that the ecumenical movement should be made up solely
of people with institutional responsibility. It must be representative of all elements within the church. It is, however, to
suggest the further development of a strategy that has been
only just begun.

Third, existing ecumenical structures should be exploited
to the full. This is not to urge that they should be enlarged into
superstructures which might, by their very size, entertain a
hope of imposing their view upon their constituencies. Not at
all. It is to urge, however, that we have as yet only glimpsed the
possibilities inherent in ecumenical organizations. To date,
they have been used for the most part in the movement upward
toward the development of ecumenical agreement of conviction. But they have not used their moral authority in request-

ing, systematically and with determination, a report by their member agencies on recommended ecumenical action. Why should they not? Is it sufficient simply to pass on to the churches a recommended action? Is it not rather irresponsible to let it go at that and not follow through to see if any action has been taken? One suspects that if ecumenical bodies developed the habit of issuing reports on the degree to which their constituent agencies had carried through in the matter of action agreed upon previously, a very considerable impetus would be given to the habit of thinking and acting ecumenically. It is, in other words, now too easy to ignore the actions of a Madras or an Amsterdam. It is as important to make people account for their actions as it is to get them to agree to take action. Should there not be an ecumenical accounting, regularly, without compulsion, but with determination?

Fourth, and perhaps most difficult, there should be developed as thoroughly as possible the habit and attitude of *learning*. Ecumenical discussions frequently convey the impression that people are there to defend positions, or heritages, or traditions, rather than to learn. No single method will insure such a spiritual change. Deeper worship at ecumenical gatherings will help. The mood and tone of ecumenical meetings, as they are set up and conducted, will help. The advance material sent to delegates and members of committees will help. Various means will need to be used, but the general object must be kept clearly in mind. One suspects that the Holy Spirit does not work most easily when a man is defending himself or his organization. One suspects that the Spirit moves with a man when his defenses are down and he is in the humble mood of seeking greater knowledge from both God and man.

It will be recognized that each of these principles is as applicable to a single congregation as it is to a denomination; to

a village council as to a national or world group of denominations. And this suggestion leads to a concluding point of ecumenical strategy. The charge is frequently leveled at national
and world organizations that they do not reach to the "grass
roots." Indeed they do not on any very important scale. They
cannot. They cannot because they do not have the money, time,
or man power. They cannot because in principle they are pre-
vented from doing so. The ecumenical concept of the church is
not a thing which can be broadcast by propaganda, however
pious or clever that propaganda may be. It is not a thing
which can be organized. It is not even a thing for which one
can whip up enthusiasm. The ecumenical concept of the church
rests upon a deep knowledge of Christ, that knowledge which
brings with it knowledge of his love and his purpose for his
church. This is something for every Christian to work out himself with his Lord. This is for those who understand it to help
others know it too. Whatever principles of ecumenical strategy
will finally prove to be effective, this much is crystal clear:
the basis of it all can only be built by those Christians, who-
ever they are, who will take the initiative themselves, because
they know the Lord.

III

We are torn by the world's divisions. Two of them eat now at
our soul's conscience. Whatever conviction we have about an
ecumenical church, it will force us to tackle the divisions of
race within the church and within the world, and the division
between the East and the West. There is much that everyone
can do about both problems, and what it is will be indicated by
the questions: In the face of what I think about these problems, and what I do about them, do I possess my integrity as a

Christian? Does the congregation I belong to possess its integrity? In white America, the unity of the ecumenical church will find its great and perhaps decisive test in its answer to these questions. In the America of capitalist democracy, the church will need to search its soul to maintain its integrity. How tragic if at this stage of ecumenical development the church in America should become simply the bulwark of western civilization, unresponsive to the Lord who stands over all civilizations!

Next steps will involve more than the ecumenical answer to these two issues. They will demand that we fully understand all of the ways in which the disunity of the surrounding society infects the church. Do economic influences rob the churches of their vitality and of their unity? Do the prevalent philosophic systems which are non-Christian or sub-Christian or anti-Christian in their presuppositions eat their way into Christian theology, affecting the springs of Christian action? If so, what is the proper response to this incursion? If we are tempted to flee, we must see the danger of that. If we are tempted to accommodate ourselves, we must realize before God what we are doing. Here is an area of the most painstaking and honest intellectual effort. Here is a next step which demands rigid honesty.

In addition, we must, especially in thinking of the unity among denominations, search out those factors in the founding and the tradition of the denominations which do not properly belong to the gospel, and we must evaluate them against the present demand for unity. We have seen the powerful effect of nationalism in the Reformation. Have elements of nationalism become a part of church tradition, and do they now keep us apart? If so, what is their true value? The individualism of the American democratic Dream has entered into our churches and

Christian thinking. Does it keep us apart, and if so, what is its value? The questions can be multiplied; one suspects that until they are multiplied and answered in all seriousness, the quest for further unity will be robbed of much of its realism.

IV

We have spoken of "our deepest difference," namely, the two fundamentally different concepts of the church and of the faith which the Amsterdam conference named as the "protestant" and the "catholic." This clearly provides the matrix out of which a whole series of steps will have to be taken. We do not know what they are to be. One clear need is for a definite understanding of just what this difference is and what it involves. If it is true that further clarification does yield two different systems of thought, is it within the realm of possibility that a solution may be found in still a third concept? These two outlooks have come down out of past tradition. They do not, as described at Amsterdam, take into account the development of the concept of the church which lies at the root of the ecumenical movement. Perhaps the great calling of the ecumenical movement is precisely at this point: to bring into these traditional concepts the leaven of yet a third which is akin to both.

On virtually every hand, there is a conviction that the great concept of the church, namely, that the church is the Body of Christ, is not a thing of words but the deepest reality. Indeed, if one had to define the ecumenical movement in a sentence, it would be that the ecumenical movement is that movement in which people of very different traditions have begun to understand the deep reality of the overarching Body of Christ. This Body gives meaning to our smaller groups; this Body provides the great ecumenical unity within which we work away at our small and our great differences alike. It is because of our knowledge of being in some sense members of this Body that, even though we feel strange with one another, we at the same time feel at home with one another. May it not be, therefore, that our deepest difference will find its ultimate resolution at just this point? Put it this way. Our deepest difference shows up at two principal points. It is a sharp difference when we discuss the continuity of our relationship with Christ, the continuity, that is, with Jesus Christ of Nazareth down through the ages and the continuity which we have with the Lord who is present now. It is a sharp difference when we discuss the fellowship which we have with each other now, and the basis upon which we can have fellowship with each other. Yet at both of these points, the reality of the Body of Christ which we are learning to know in the ecumenical movement rises up and goes beyond even these differences. We have a sense of continuity in the Body of Christ and we have a sense of fellowship in the Body of Christ, which though they cannot be clearly defined and agreed to, nevertheless capture our minds and hold our allegiance. Time and again ecumenical gatherings acknowledge unity in Christ and turn right around and make dogmatic affirmations which seem to shatter that unity. Yet that unity is not shattered by these dogmatic affirmations. Must we not therefore work together upon the substance of what we have been given, to see whether there is not in the greater reality of the Body of Christ something which is deeper than even our deepest difference? If we had only two conceptions of the church to go on, the "protestant" and the "catholic," we would be in a bad situation. In fact, we have been given a third. Is not the way ahead to work on the meaning of this third reality, which is in fact the greatest of all?

The third World Conference on Faith and Order, held in the summer of 1952 in Lund, Sweden, dealt with this third reality in a way which gives large promise for future unity. In a very real sense, the Lund Conference departed from the traditions of its two predecessor Faith and Order meetings. They had found it necessary, and as we have seen, extremely valuable, to explore the differences and the agreements of the various traditions, laying them, as it were, side by side, to see where the real difference and agreement lay. This made it possible for the churches to understand where they stood in relation to one another, and to engage in true ecumenical discussion. At Amsterdam, it was found that behind these specific agreements and differences there lay the "deepest difference."

At the Lund Conference it was understood that behind the present position of the churches there also lies a profound unity. Rather than again list the agreements and differences, the Report of the Lund Conference deals with this great, unifying ground upon which all the churches rest. "Jesus Christ is the King of the new People of God. 'He is the chief cornerstone in which the whole building, fitly framed together, grows up into a holy temple in the Lord.' He is the Head of the Church which is his Body. Through his Spirit, Jesus Christ himself is present in his Church. Christ lives in his Church and the Church lives in Christ. Christ is never without his Church; the Church is never without Christ" (*Third World Conference on Faith and Order, Official Report,* Chapter II). If therefore there is to be any progress in unity, a special need exists to examine the relationship between Christ and the church. The point was clearly seen that, useful as it is for certain purposes to examine the relationship between various churches, the real point of further progress toward unity is to discover together the relationship which in fact exists between Him who has created all of the churches, and those churches themselves. This is the key, as the third chapter of the *Report* points out, to the vexed problems of unity and of continuity as well. "The Pauline image of the Church as the Body of Christ is no mere metaphor, but expresses a living reality. All agree in finding the presence of Jesus Christ, the crucified and risen Lord, both living in and reigning over his Church. She is created as the realm of redemption by the sovereign grace of God and is also the sphere of His acts of judgment and reformation. We unite in affirming the solidarity between the Head and the members and also the sovereignty of the Head over the members in the Body of Christ" (*Report*, Chapter III).

Behind this insistence upon the supremacy of Jesus Christ over the churches lie two increasingly important trends. One of these is a sharp awareness of the influence of social factors upon the life and thought of the denominations. In recent years, many Christian brethren from behind the Iron Curtain have brought about a clearer recognition of the importance of social forces of all kinds upon our Christian thinking and behavior. For them, under the pressure of the new regime, the problem has been to discover the point at which Christian faith in its deepest and purest form must part company with ecclesiastical, political, and social ideas of the past. Many in Germany faced virtually the same issue under the Nazi regime. The effect of this process has been to force men to try to lift Jesus Christ up high, seeing him as he is, stripped of traditional vestments. Many mistakes have of course been made. But those who fight this battle insist that Christ can be seen in this stark way, and their conviction is forcing those who are concerned with the unity of the church, to try to penetrate behind their traditional concepts in order that for the sake of unity, we may be led by

Christ alone. Experience under persecution and under pressure
has been reinforced by the work of a number of scholars who
have shown that in successive ages the churches tend to take on
the coloration of the thought-world and the social milieu in
which they live. Historical knowledge joins therefore with present experience to lead Christians of many traditions to seek
their Lord afresh.

A second trend which has had the same result is the growing
recognition of the importance of an eschatological view of the
Christian faith. Such a view looks forward, as the chief element
in the Christian hope, to the time when God will establish his
Kingdom, and when the victory of Christ over the powers of
evil will be complete. Here again the testimony of people who
are subjected to the suffering of persecution, war, and human
hopelessness for the future is of particular value to those of us
who live in a still secure and powerful land where freedom exists in great measure. With successive political regimes wiping
out all that men held dear in civilization, with the future of
civilization threatened in the most drastic way by the after-
maths of two wars and the fearsome prospect of a third, these
Christians have been forced to ask themselves, on the deepest
level, what there is that can be held to be a sure hope. Out of
the anguish of their souls has come the conviction that there
is nothing sure but God, that hope for the future lies in the
assurance he has given that his Kingdom will come and that
his will shall be done. This knowledge and the hope which is
born out of it provides an immensely powerful motive force
for life now: it keeps life going and it keeps men fighting the
battle for Christ against evil. It also provides a framework in
which to view the evil of the disunity. The church "continues
to be a pilgrim people in a strange land, so that all its life and
work on earth is incomplete. Ungodly powers and forces are

still rampant in the whole creation in an alarming way, and they seek to confuse the church and defeat its mission. But the church continues to live and work by the power of Jesus Christ. "At the end of its pilgrimage Jesus Christ, the Crucified and Risen, will come again to meet his Church in order to complete his work of redemption and judgment. Out of all peoples and ages he will gather his own who look for his appearing and for a new heaven and a new earth, and he will consummate the union between Christ and his Church in the eternal kingdom of God" (*Report*, Chapter II).

Such a perspective upon the faith makes many of our differences seem small and inconsequential. When Christ is lifted up, all men are drawn unto him. The conclusion for the matter of church unity is clear: "When we place ourselves in our churches under his judgment and in obedience to his calling and his sending, we shall know that we cannot manifest our unity and share in his fullness without being changed. . . . Those who are ever looking backward and have accumulated much precious ecclesiastical baggage will perhaps be shown that pilgrims must travel light and that if we are to share at last in the great Supper, we must let go much of that treasure" (*Report*, Chapter II).

How we travel light, we do not know. Jesus Christ is the Lord, and he is the Head of the church. It is clear that each of our now separated churches, and all of them together, must be put in the right relationship to Him, so that he becomes in fact the *Lord* over all. It is clear that we are at the threshold of the very fundamentals, at that point where Christians must always walk in faith and trust. The next step will be to walk in this fashion, facing with honesty whatever obstacle may be in the way.

In the meantime, the existence of this deepest difference—
"protestant" and "catholic"—has important implications for
unity in the United States. As we have noted, the great block
of American protestantism is "radical" or "free" protestantism, the Reformed, Lutheran, and Anglican and the Orthodox
elements in the scene being relatively small, and even at that
strongly influenced by the free church tradition. The most crucial problems of unity do not appear, in the American scene,
in their most forceful forms. For this reason we are likely to be
misled into thinking that Christian unity is easier to achieve
than it actually is. The homogeneity of American Christianity,
its still prevailing disinterest in theological questions, and the
absence in any strong measure of traditions which sharply challenge the majority consensus are likely to betray us into superficiality. Indeed, one suspects that this has already happened in
some measure. It is to be noted, with regret, that the councils
of churches in the United States, city, state, and national, do
not have departments dealing with the differences and the unity
of the churches as such. Departments of evangelism, religious
education, social action, public relations, worship, and others
exist. Departments of faith and order are lacking. Is this testimony to be an existing superficiality in our approach to unity?
Some will argue that it is not, that there is no need to raise un-
necessary questions where they do not exist. If there is a homogeneity of outlook, why not capitalize on it? One suspects that
this is too easy an answer, and that there must be some deep
mind-searching and soul-searching concerning our faith. Co-
operation based upon profound thinking together is one thing;
co-operation based upon too easy assumptions concerning faith
and conviction is another. One major next step for the movement toward unity in the United States may well be a deepening of the theological basis upon which our co-operative

movements rest, and a searching out of what co-operation means, in its full implications.

On the asset side of our question, we have said that the ecumenical movement is established, and with power; and that there is self-criticism and renewal in the churches. These in one sense all go together, and they pose a question for each Christian which must sooner or later be faced. Is this ecumenical movement of God or is it not? Many, adopting Gamaliel's advice, are simply waiting to see, standing by for that time when the movement shall become so unmistakably powerful that it will catch them up without effort or cost on their part. They will have their reward. Others face this question now. We believe that it is no longer necessary to wait, that the evidence is abundant that it is a movement born of God and desired by him.

If this is true, it forces another direct question to every Christian. What is my attitude to be toward it? If this movement is of God, am I the kind of Christian which fits into the emerging pattern? The question is directed primarily toward one's convictions about the church. What is the church? If the ecumenical movement has done nothing else, it has asked that question with such insistence that no one can now escape it. We may say that the church is not the Body of Christ, but the body of some Apollos. At least we are forced to give that answer. We may say that the church is the Body of Christ, and with our statement be forced to another fact, namely, that unity among Christians matters, and matters desperately. If the ecumenical movement is of God, we are driven to attack our deepest differences in love, in understanding, and with determination—wherever we may be able to attack them. We are driven for the love of God and for the love of man and for the love of the church to strike and strike again at the divisions of society and of race which separate man from man. We will be driven to boldness of strategy. We will be driven to a true concept of the church, held with such depth that it animates all of our days and hours.

Yet, we are beset with a great danger. A pattern of unity has been established in the world, in the nations, in the towns and cities. We co-operate with each other. The danger is that we yield too much to the comfort of co-operation, and that this pattern may become static. It would be so easy now to settle back and work away at perfecting the procedures, analyzing the problems, carrying on the day-to-day business. Satisfied with the participation of the leaders of the churches, the ecumenical agencies may slide by the full awakening of the churches themselves.

It will always be the next step to keep the drive to unity alive, to prevent the ecumenical movement from slipping into comfortable and ineffective habits. How can it be done? Not by human efforts alone. It can be done only by ceaseless vigilance, under the Lord and in the Lord. Under the Lord, in the sense that we must always seek his judgment upon what we have done and now do. In the Lord, in the sense that his love is the only eternal and ultimately powerful force. And with ceaseless vigilance in the sense of the Scripture: *Be ye therefore like men who wait for their master to return.*

PART TWO

*The movement toward unity, as we have been con-
cerned to point out, must effectively engage the churches.
It is therefore of the highest importance that we know
those families of churches which are involved in seeking
closer unity with one another. The following statements,
each written by a leader of the respective communions,
are provided to help achieve this end.*

*It has been impossible to include statements concern-
ing all of the Protestant and Orthodox churches in the
United States. The following, however, represent most
of them, and provide a view of the distinctive witness of
the great branches of the Christian communions which
are at work together in the ecumenical movement.*

ANNA CANADA SWAIN

Baptists

There are in the world today about eighteen million Baptists, of which over fourteen million live in the United States. The largest group in America is found in the Southern Baptist Convention, which now numbers over seven million. The National Baptist Convention, Incorporated, claims over four million, and the American Baptist Convention over one and a half million.

Robert G. Torbet writes in "What Baptists Believe":

Baptists share with other Christians the great doctrines of the faith. They believe in the triune God, the Father, Son, and Holy Spirit; they teach that Jesus Christ is God in the flesh, the Lord and Saviour of all who will confess their sins and receive Him by faith; they accept the responsibility set forth in the Great Commission of giving the gospel message to the whole world. But Baptists also have a special witness to bear before their fellow Christians and the world. It is this "Baptist witness" which gives them their distinctive character.

Historically, Baptists stem from the Anabaptists of the sixteenth century, a group which were abused and criticized as revolutionaries, heretics, and fanatics. Without in any way belittling the religious contributions of Luther and Calvin, Baptists today believe that these left-wing Anabaptists watered with their martyred blood the seeds of new and important ideas. These ideas flowered in the sects of the seventeenth century and are influential in the thinking of the free church group of the twentieth century.

Today, when human liberty and freedom of speech are so often threatened, the Anabaptists of the sixteenth century may be recognized as pioneers in the idea of a "free society." It was from within this group of radicals that there came the then revolutionary idea of religious toleration. They insisted that force should not be used in matters of religion and conscience, and that neither church nor state should compel men to accept uniformity of belief or practice.

This emphasis on the importance of individual decision has resulted in groups of Baptists around the world, who vary in some respects but are united on certain principles.

Perhaps the two greatest differences to be found in the United States are:

1. American Baptists and National Baptists, Incorporated, feel that they may work in good conscience with interdenominational and ecumenical groups, while Southern Baptists feel that they cannot.

2. American and National Baptists are much less strict than are Southern Baptists in accepting into church membership those who have not been immersed in their own churches. In most cases, this is provided through "associate membership." In recent years, some churches have adopted "open membership."

Baptists around the world, however, are practically unanimous on the following beliefs and practices:

1. The Local Church

While Baptist churches co-operate voluntarily in associations, and state and national conventions, they lay great emphasis on the supreme autonomy of the local church and maintain that the local church has no earthly superior. They believe in a congregational form of government and use such forms and methods as are not forbidden in the Scriptures. They summarize the functions of the local church, after a careful study of the Acts and the Epistles, under four headings: (1) regulation of the membership; (2) elections of its officers; (3) maintenance of worship and the ordinances; (4) general management and dispensing of relief. The practical working out of these functions means that the first and third come under the care of the deacons, function two is the responsibility of the entire church, and function four comes under a board of trustees or executive committee.

The ordinance of the Lord's Supper is observed in the local church as a memorial of Jesus Christ. When a Communion service is held in a group larger than the local church, it is held at the invitation of a local church and is considered the Communion service of that local church. A large number of Baptist churches invite all who love the Lord Jesus Christ and accept him as their Saviour, to partake at his table.

2. The Member of a Baptist Church

a) Baptists do not believe in infant baptism. In their opinion, an individual must have a personal experience of the regenerative work of the Holy Spirit as a pre-requisite of church membership.

b) Experience of a changed life should be followed by "believer's baptism," which almost always means baptism by immersion. While some Baptists have practiced other forms of baptism, the symbolism of the dying to sin and the resurrection to a new life in Christ is generally accepted. However, Baptists do not believe that the form has any saving power of itself.

c) Baptists believe that it is essential to accept the Bible as the supreme authority in their daily living. They believe it should be read systematically and that each individual should interpret it for himself without any coercion.

d) Baptists do not subscribe to any creed, but accept the New Testament as their guide for living a Christian life. From time to time, certain statements of basic Christian truths have been made but these are never imposed on others. The two principal confessions (Philadelphia Confession, 1689, and New Hampshire Confession, 1832) are not complete statements of Baptist beliefs, nor are they binding.

e) Baptists believe also in the priesthood of the believer; for they feel that each believer receives salvation and has free access to God at any time for spiritual comfort and for forgiveness of his sins through Jesus Christ, our Lord and Saviour.

3. *The Baptist Pastor*

Because of their belief in the priesthood of each believer, there is equality between clergy and laity. The pastor is simply one member of the church who is on an equal footing with other members. The result is that the worship services conducted by pastors have little ritual and are more informal than in many churches. Ministers are licensed to preach by the churches where they are members. When ordination is desired, the candidate is brought before a council called by the candidate's church, which is composed of members of sister churches. At this council, the candidate is questioned regarding his call to the ministry, his experience, and his beliefs. He becomes a member of the church of which he is pastor and shares with the deacons and other elected officers of the church the responsibilities of his office. He, with all other members, is under the discipline of the church.

4. Religious Liberty and Separation of Church and State

The most distinctive belief of Baptists has been the principle of religious liberty. In this matter, Baptists stood practically alone until the nineteenth century. This belief is the natural result of the scriptural teaching of the individual's responsibility to God alone. Consequently, Baptists have, for over three hundred years, defended the right of both individuals and groups to believe in God or disbelieve in him. Roger Williams and John Clarke in the State of Rhode Island and Providence Plantations in the early 1600's laid such emphasis on this matter that one hundred and fifty years later, references to religious tests and restrictions were omitted from our national Constitution.

A natural corollary of this idea is found in the principle of the separation of church and state. In this matter, Baptists have insisted that the state has no right to interfere with the religious beliefs and practices of individuals or churches, and also that the churches should not accept financial aid from the state.

5. Conclusion

Baptists believe that by following the above principles, the spiritual vitality of the New Testament church may be preserved.

R. NORRIS WILSON

❧❧

The Congregational Christian Churches

The Congregational Church in America "landed" with the Pilgrims in New England. Its faith and order are rooted in the insistence of the Pilgrims and Puritans that the local congregation has liberties under God which no civil or ecclesiastical superior can remove. This is based upon the conviction that a true congregation is always "gathered" by Christ, and his voice is likely to be more clearly heard there than when mediated through other authorities. The history of the Plymouth and Massachusetts Bay Colonies and the history of Congregationalism, therefore, are closely interwoven, and the names of Bradford, Cotton, Standish, Brewster, and Winthrop are as significant to the tradition of the churches as to the early history of the nation.

The Congregational Christian Churches * stand in the Reformed tradition. It was, in fact, the exalted position of the

---

* The name "Christian" was brought into the official title of the denomination by the "Christian Church," which had its beginnings in the United States in the late eighteenth century and merged with the Congregational Churches in 1931.

Bible as the gift of a Sovereign God—so central to the thought
of Calvin—which was in large part the inspiration of Congregationalism.

The churches have no official creed in the sense that there
is today a written standard of faith and practice. There is no
creedal test for membership. Because this is so, there have
been many attempts to express the belief of the churches, and
while having no official creed the Congregationalists have been
great creed makers.

The main lines of Congregational faith and practice are to
be found in the Westminster Confession, the Cambridge Platform and, more recently, the Kansas City Statement adopted in
1913.

The latter Statement reads in part as follows:

> . . . declaring the steadfast allegiance of the churches com-
> posing the Council to the faith which our fathers confessed,
> which from age to age has found its expression in the his-
> toric creeds of the church universal and of this communion,
> and affirming our loyalty to the basic principles of our
> representative democracy, hereby set forth the things most
> surely believed among us concerning faith, polity, and fel-
> lowship:

Faith

We believe in God the Father, infinite in wisdom, good-
ness and love; and in Jesus Christ, his Son, our Lord and
Saviour, who for us and our salvation lived and died and
rose again and liveth evermore; and in the Holy Spirit, who
taketh of the things of Christ and revealeth them to us, re-
newing, comforting, and inspiring the souls of men. We are
united in striving to know the will of God as taught in the

Holy Scriptures, and to our purpose to walk in the ways of the Lord, made known or to be made known to us. We hold it to be the mission of the Church of Christ to proclaim the gospel to all mankind, exalting the worship of the one true God and laboring for the progress of knowledge, the promotion of justice, the reign of peace, and the realization of human brotherhood. Depending, as did our fathers, upon the continued guidance of the Holy Spirit to lead us into all truth, we work and pray for the transformation of the world into the kingdom of God; and we look with faith for the triumph of righteousness and the life everlasting.

There are three ruling ideas which, while not unique to Congregationalism, are persistently characteristic of its faith and life.

First, the Bible is the primary rule of faith and practice. Taking full account of modern biblical scholarship, the literalism of earlier days is rarely present in the church, but it is the Scriptures, as interpreted under the guidance of the Holy Spirit, upon which the churches chiefly rely for leading in all matters. Early Congregationalists reasoned that if the Bible were a sufficient guide in all things for personal and social life, it ought also to provide guidance for the life and practice of the church. It was this conviction that produced the characteristic Congregational Polity.

Secondly, Congregationalists believe that what distinguishes between an assembly of Christian people and a church is that the members of a congregation are united into a church by a "willing covenant" made with their God. "A company becomes a church by joyning in Covenant" (R. Mather). This is not always or necessarily a formal expression of the church's faith, but it is always present, at least implicitly. According to the principle of the covenant, it is only church members, and not bishops or other officers, who, acting in Christ's name, admit new members to the church. "We conceive the real substance of it [the covenant] is kept where there is a real agreement and consent of a company of faithful persons to meet constantly together in one congregation for the public worship of God and their mutual edification" (Cambridge Platform).

Thirdly, the doctrine of the Holy Spirit has a central place in the faith and life of the church. The guidance of the Holy Spirit is not conceived as private illumination by the "inner light," but rather the near and present leading of God in Christ, through the Holy Spirit who, according to the promise "will lead you into all truth." The presence of Christ to his people in the church, gathered at worship or in the church meeting, is the assured presence of the Holy Spirit. It is the Holy Spirit, the comforter and guide, that leads the church to its understanding of Scripture, and tradition. And it is the Holy Spirit who guides and "prevents" the individual, through his membership, toward a righteous and faithful life.

Order

The Congregational Christian Fellowship is by no means the only denomination having "congregational order." The Baptists and Disciples, for example, are "congregational" denominations. The distinguishing feature of this form of church government is the authority of the local congregation. In the Congregational denomination there are two principles by which the affairs of the churches are disposed: freedom of the local congregation from the rule of any authority save Christ himself; and fellowship, which is the association of one church with another and with their denominational organizations for the advancement of their common tasks.

These two principles of freedom and fellowship appear to be contradictory, but in actual practice they are complementary. The freedom of the local church gives a heightened meaning to the work of the fellowship as a whole. More than this, the fact that the churches are free from ecclesiastical control and subject only to the Lordship of Christ has given to Congregational churchmanship a depth and range which is characteristic. It is true to say that the activity of the denomination in the fields of higher education, the social application of Christianity, and ecumenical affairs is traceable to this twofold principle of freedom and fellowship. The theory is summed up in the words of the Cambridge Platform:

> Although churches be distinct, and therefore may not be confounded one with another; and equal, and therefore have not dominion one over another; yet all the churches ought to preserve church-communion one with another.

Again, while it may appear that the unlimited freedom of the local congregation could be a handicap to the life of the fellowship, in fact, the claims of the fellowship counterbalance the temptations of unlimited freedom, so that the two principles of freedom and fellowship provide what is virtually a system of "checks and balances" in the life of the church.

Organization

Every church is a member of an Association, which is a group of churches varying in size from twenty to one hundred churches. It is the Association which in many cases ordains to the ministry and which holds the standing of its ministerial members. Churches are represented in the Association by elected delegates. The Association ordinarily meets twice each year. Except in matters of church and ministerial standing, its decisions are only advisory in relation to the churches which compose it, but no church or minister who lacks the approval of an Association holds standing in the denomination.

The Conference is the largest unit of the Fellowship in which each church has representation. The Conferences are for the most part State Conferences, although some Conferences include all or parts of more than one state. The Conference is a corporate body with a superintendent and staff. It unites the churches in a concerted program for church extension, religious education, and other undertakings which may become the churches' responsibility together. The Conference is both the promotional and receiving agency for the cultivation of missionary education and giving.

The national organization is officially known as the General Council of the Congregational Christian Churches in the U.S.A. It is a voluntary organization of the Congregational Christian Churches, made up of representatives elected by neighborhood units of church members numbering a thousand or more. The General Council meets every two years, the purpose of its meeting being to provide a gathering for useful discussion of questions related to the larger life of the Fellowship.

It is the purpose of the General Council to foster and express the substantial unity of the Congregational Christian Churches in faith, purpose, polity, and work; to consult upon and devise measures and maintain agencies for the promotion of the common interests of the kingdom of God.

Statistics

There are 5,651 churches belonging to the Congregational Christian Fellowship in the United States. A total membership of these churches is 1,227,527.

The largest concentration of Congregational Christian Churches is in the New England area, although the "center" of Congregational population is in the area of Cleveland, Ohio.

IRA W. LANGSTON

❧❦❧

Disciples of Christ

The churches of the Disciples of Christ are Christian communities which began to take form organizationally on the frontiers of the North American Continent in the days when the new democratic society, which has since become the United States, was being forged from forests and freedom, disasters and daring, hopes and hardships, by the pioneers who settled here. To understand this movement, one would best view it through the four influences that have had the most to do with molding and tempering its formation.

In the first instance, the men and women who organized and gave direction to these churches were Christians from the evangelical Protestant tradition. They accepted the "gospel of Christ as the power of God unto the salvation of souls." They believed that the church is the "Body of Christ." They were churchmen who were acquainted with the Bible as the only source book of authority for faith and practice, both in the church and for their daily lives. Many of them were ordained clergymen, trained in some of the best universities and seminaries of the "old countries." There was no disposition on their

142

part to rewrite or even to redefine the basic theological and ecclesiastical tenets of the church. These they rejected as not being authoritative. There was certainly no disposition on their part to organize another church. They were evangelical Protestant Christians faced with a new and strange social situation, and they sought to make the church and the Christ available and vital for themselves and their neighbors in this situation.

The second influence follows naturally upon the first. They were living on a frontier. In this situation, the individuals who survived were competent and responsible. There were few specialists. Few people had a disposition to depend on the decisions of others. On their ability to decide and act responsibly in a wide variety of situations rested their hope for survival. They built their own homes, doctored their own ills, and prayed their own prayers. Under such conditions, one would expect them to organize their own churches, raise up and ordain their own clergy, and analyze (to accept or reject) their own doctrine—which they did.

How did they do these things? By what authority? They were limited in their assumption of responsibility for themselves only by the Bible, especially the New Testament, and the majority vote of the congregation. The congregation was the highest court of appeal except in matters cleary defined in the text of the New Testament. On this frontier these responsible individuals read their New Testaments, and under this inspiration they used the resources at their disposal to organize their own churches.

The third influence, again following with equal naturalness, which tempered the formation and direction of the Disciples of Christ was the matter of Christian unity. The frontier was sparsely populated. The pioneers longed for fellowship. They hungered for it, both for the presence of God and for the company of their neighbors. Such is understandable. And yet the churches on the frontier were as likely to be sources of conflict and separation as sources of unity and fellowship. Scarcely did a group of pioneers find that they all happened to belong to the same communion. So that most blessed fellowship, the society of brothers and sisters gathered in communion with the Spirit of God through Jesus Christ, was denied the frontier community almost altogether.

It was doubtless for this reason that the Christian Association of Washington, Pennsylvania, under the leadership of Thomas Campbell, an ordained Presbyterian clergyman, adopted "The Declaration and Address," which says among other things, "Division among Christians is a horrid evil, fraught with many evils." In another place, this same document says, "The Church of Christ upon the earth is essentially, intentionally, and constitutionally one."

The Disciples of Christ have made such a witness in every pronouncement from that day to this. They have had and continue to have a passion for Christian unity.

The fourth and final of these influences which have made the Disciples what they are is their emphasis upon "Restoration." Under the banner of this word the churches and preachers of the Disciples of Christ have sought to lead a return to the New Testament to find what the "true" and "sacred" order of the church is and should be. The pattern of the "Primitive Church" has been the source of a great search among these people. Much that has been of doubtful value has been taught and disputed because these democratically governed and autonomous Christian communities have failed to agree on the exact definition of the "divine plan in the Primitive Church."

But interestingly enough and particularly pertinent in such a study as this, their attempt to find the pattern of the early church was not an end in and of itself. This, I think, is unique. The Disciples have sought the "New Testament order of Things" for the church, not so they could be *right*, but as the basis for the unity of the church of Jesus Christ. They have sought this divine plan, not in the history or traditions of Christendom, not in the great pronouncements of church councils, but in the New Testament.

In a frontier situation where much of the ancient pronouncements and doctrines was scarcely relevant, where ecclesiastical structure and priestly functions were impossible, where sparse population and differences of opinion made fellowship unavailable, these Christian pioneers organized themselves into "Christian Associations" dedicated to the union of the Church of Jesus Christ, which they sought to make available by locating and understanding the New Testament precedent and by "restoring" that "plan" in the faith and practice of at least one Christian community of congregations.

In the light of these things, let us make some summary observations on the position of the Disciples of Christ.

1. There is no written creed nor is there any authoritative statement of a body of doctrine which defines the faith and practice of the Disciples of Christ. There is not even a means whereby such a doctrinal position could be taken if such a procedure should become desirable. The New Testament is the authoritative statement of faith and practice, and the local congregation has the power and the responsibility for interpreting the Scriptures in all matters of faith and worship for its own constituency. Such action should be taken under the counsel of the elders and by the vote of the congregation. Creeds and other materials are not rejected as wholly evil, but no capital is made by condemning theology. Creeds may be used for

teaching, but they cannot (by tradition) be used for excluding anyone from the fellowship of any congregation.

Uniformity of opinion is not the goal. Unity of spirit in a humble search for the will of God is much more to be desired. The search centers in the New Testament. The church is a community of Christians, in search of the will of God through Jesus Christ as revealed in the New Testament.

2. Membership in a congregation of the Disciples of Christ is usually achieved by the convert when he confesses and accepts "Jesus Christ as the Son of God and his personal Saviour" and is baptized by immersion. Following these acts of personal identification and acceptance by the candidate, he becomes a full and active communicant of the church. No other statement of faith will ever be required of him. No doctrinal position he may take can be the cause for his dismissal.

Baptism by immersion is universally held and practiced by congregations of the Disciples. It was accepted by the early congregations solely on the strength of their understanding (and voting) that it was the New Testament practice. While immersion would be essential for converts in this communion, they would not refuse fellowship with others of different practices.

3. The weekly worship experience of the congregation (usually Sunday morning) centers about the Communion of the Lord's Supper. This is a service of the beloved community, conducted usually by lay elders, elected from and ordained by the congregation. The emblems are considered symbols, but the experience of the individual and of the community is held to be completely divine. Here, as in no other act or thought, is the confrontation of the human by the living Spirit of Jesus Christ. The service is what may be called "open," in that each

individual is called upon to examine himself and partake accordingly.

In this matter, as with baptism by immersion, the Disciples of Christ would scarcely insist that every person and church follow their practice, but they would resist through extreme measures any who would seek to deprive them of this regular weekly observance.

4. The primary unit of the Disciples of Christ is the baptized believer with the New Testament in his hand. These are voluntarily associated into local congregations which have cooperatively established state, national, and world organizations (conventions, missionary societies, publishing houses, educational institutions, benevolent associations, evangelistic associations, and the like) for the purpose of sustaining and extending the Kingdom of God through Jesus Christ across the face of the earth. Currently, there are 8,249 congregations serving 1,945,607 communicants in the United States and Canada.

Every Disciple individual and congregation should, if true to the traditions, rejoice and thank God for every extension of fellowship, for the downfall of any and every barrier that excludes one or more followers of Christ from Communion with their Lord in the company of His Church.

ARCHBISHOP MICHAEL *

❧

The Eastern Orthodox Church

The Orthodox Church is a democratic body which comprises, first, churches founded by the Apostles themselves, or by the disciples of the Apostles, and which have remained in full communion with one another; and secondly, those churches which have derived their origin from the missionary activity of the first churches, or which were founded by separation from them, without loss of communion.

To the first class belong the four Patriarchates of Constantinople, Alexandria, Antioch, and Jerusalem, and the Church of Cyprus. The Church of Constantinople was founded by St. Andrew, and the Church of Alexandria by St. Mark, the Church of Antioch by St. Paul, the Church of Jerusalem by St. Peter and St. James, and the Church of Cyprus by St. Paul and St. Barnabas.

To the second class belong the Church of Sinai, the Church of Russia, the Church of Greece, the Church of Serbia, the Church of Romania, the Church of Georgia in the Caucasus, the Church of Poland, and the Church of Albania.

---

* of the GREEK ORTHODOX CHURCH of North and South America.

The two World Wars and the resulting national and political changes have left their mark in many alterations in various churches of Orthodoxy.

Most of the Orthodox churches have branches in the United States, headed by a Bishop or an Archbishop under the spiritual jurisdiction of the Mother Church in their ancestral homelands.

According to a recent survey of the National Council of the Churches of Christ in the U.S.A., the various branches of the Orthodox Church in the United States have about three million members. The Greek and Russian branches are the largest.

All these churches are independent of each other in their administration, but at the same time are in full communion with one another. What is more important, and must be strongly emphasized, they have the same faith, doctrine, apostolic tradition, sacraments, liturgies, and holy services.

Among the Orthodox people of all these churches, there is no difference arising from the ecclesiastical authority to which they give allegiance. The only essential thing for them is the Orthodox Church and the Orthodox faith. For this very reason, if one goes to Russia, Romania, Serbia, and asks the people to which church they belong, they will not answer that they belong to the Russian, the Romanian, or the Serbian Church, but to the Greek Orthodox Church. The churches are national, but these national churches are in brotherly fellowship. Together they constitute Orthodoxy. Together they honor, as first among equals, the occupant of the Ecumenical Throne of Constantinople.

The Orthodox Church derives her teaching from two sources: the Holy Scriptures and the Sacred Tradition. These two sources, according to the Orthodox conviction, are of equal value and they complete each other. The Orthodox Church regards the Sacred Tradition as an essential complement of Holy Scripture, because the Apostles wrote the various books which constitute the New Testament from different motives; consequently, it is impossible that the Holy Scriptures should contain all the teachings of our Lord and his Apostles, which at the beginning were transmitted orally. Therefore, Sacred Tradition is older than the New Testament.

Sacred Tradition includes the doctrines of the Faith and the Sacraments with their attendant ritual, as transmitted from one generation of the faithful to another both by word and example. It is embodied in the decrees and definitions of the Seven Ecumenical Councils, in the Niceo-Constantinopolitan Creed, in the writings of the Holy Fathers of the undivided church (which is usually reckoned as closing with St. John of Damascus), and in the decrees and definitions of certain later Synods and Councils.

The basic faith of the Orthodox Church is expressed in the words of the Niceo-Constantinopolitan Creed, which is the only one recited at the baptism of every new member and at the celebration of every Liturgy.

The Orthodox Church believes that God is One in substance and Trinity in persons. It worships One God in Trinity, and Trinity in Unity, neither confusing the persons nor dividing the substance. The Creation is the work in time of the Blessed Trinity. The world is not self-created, neither has it existed from eternity, but it is the product of the wisdom, the power, and the will of One God in Trinity. God the Father is the prime cause of the Creation, and God the Son and God the Holy Ghost took part in the Creation, God the Son perfecting the Creation and God the Holy Ghost vivifying the Creation.

The Orthodox Church believes that our Lord Jesus Christ is

truly God. He is Jesus, that is, the Saviour and Christ, the Lord's Anointed, a Son not created of another substance, as is the case with us, but a Son begotten of the very substance of the Father before all time, and thus consubstantial with the Father. He is also truly man, like us in every respect, except sin. The denial either of His divinity or of His humanity constitutes a denial of His incarnation and of our salvation. The Holy Spirit proceeds from the Father. The faith of the church about the procession of the Holy Spirit was confirmed by the Second Ecumenical Council, which added to the Creed the following clause: "And I believe in the Holy Spirit, the Lord, the Giver of Life, who proceedeth from the Father."

The church is the holy institution founded by our Lord Jesus Christ for the salvation of men, bearing His holy sanction and authority, and composed of men having one and the same faith, and partaking of the same sacraments. It is divided into the clergy and laity. The clergy trace their descent by uninterrupted succession from the Apostles, and through them from our Lord Jesus Christ. The church is one because our Lord Jesus Christ founded not many, but only one church; holy because her aim, the sanctification and salvation of her members through the sacraments, is holy; catholic because she is above local limitations; and apostolic because she was "built upon the foundation of the Apostles, Jesus Christ himself being the chief cornerstone" (Eph. 2:20). The Head of the church is our Lord Jesus Christ.

The Orthodox Church recognizes seven sacraments: Baptism, Chrism or Confirmation, Holy Eucharist, Confession, Ordination, Marriage, and Holy Unction. Baptism is the door through which one enters into the church. Confirmation is the completion of baptism. In the sacrament of the Holy Eucharist, under the kinds of bread and wine, we partake of the very Body and the very Blood of our Lord Jesus Christ for remission of sins and eternal life. Both the New Testament and Sacred Tradition bear witness to the real presence of our Lord in the Holy Eucharist. In the sacrament of Confession, Jesus Christ, the founder of the sacrament, through the confessor, forgives the sins committed after baptism by the person who confesses his sins and sincerely repents for them. In the sacrament of Ordination, through prayer and the laying-on of hands by a bishop, Divine Grace comes down on the ordained, enabling him to be a worthy minister of the church. Apostolic succession is fundamental to the church. Without it the church is quite unthinkable. In the sacrament of Marriage, Divine Grace sanctifies the union of husband and wife. In the sacrament of Holy Unction, the sick person is anointed with sanctified oil and Divine Grace heals both his bodily and spiritual ills.

At death, man's body goes to the earth from which it was taken, and the soul, being immortal, goes to God, who gave it. The souls of men, being conscious and exercising all their faculties immediately after death, are judged by God. This judgment following man's death we call the Particular Judgment. The final reward of men, however, we believe will take place at the time of the General Judgment, which is called the Intermediate State, the souls of men having a foretaste of their blessing or punishment.

Further, the Orthodox Church venerates and honors the Saints and asks their intercession with God, but it adores and worships God the Father and the Son and the Holy Spirit. Of all Saints, it honors exceedingly the Mother of our Lord, because of the supreme grace and the call which she received from God. Though she was not exempt from original sin, from which she was cleansed at the time of the Annunciation, we believe that by the Grace of God she did not commit any actual sin. The church venerates the sacred ikons and relics. Yet this veneration, according to the decisions and canons of the Seventh Ecumenical Council, relates not to the sacred images as such, but to their prototypes, the persons whom they represent.

The Orthodox Church has three orders of ministry: deacons, priests, and bishops. The deacons assist in the work of the parish and in the service of the sacraments. Priests and deacons are of two orders: secular and monastic. Marriage is allowed to the candidates for the diaconate and priesthood, but it is forbidden after ordination. As a rule, the episcopate is confined to members of the monastic order. The parishes are generally in the care of secular priests.

Monks and nuns are gathered in monastic establishments. In some of these the members live in communities, while in others they lead a secluded, hermitical life, each in his own cell. There is but one order, and the vows are the same for all: obedience, chastity, prayer, fasting, and poverty.

The organization for the general government of the different Orthodox churches varies in different countries. In general, there is a Council, at the head of which, as president, is a bishop elected by the ecclesiastical representatives of the people. Historically, and in some cases even at the present, this presiding bishop is called the "Patriarch." The largest or most important of the bishoprics connected with the Patriarchate, or Synod, are called "Metropolitan sees," although this title now carries with it no special ecclesiastical authority.

JOSEPH SITTLER

᠊ᢀᡄᢓᡂᢂ

The Lutheran Churches

The Lutheran churches, the oldest non-Roman churches in western Christendom, trace their beginnings as self-conscious bodies of believers to the time of the Reformation of the sixteenth century. The symbols everywhere recognized as descriptive of Lutheranism's understanding of Christianity are the Ecumenical Creeds, the Catechism of Martin Luther (1529), and the Augsburg Confession (1530). Some national churches within the Lutheran family assign confessional status also to the following: the Apology of the Augsburg Confession, the Smalkald Articles (1537), the Formula of Concord (1580).

Lutheranism acknowledges as its theological basis, the standard by which all teaching is to be judged, the Word of God supremely manifested in Jesus Christ and incomparably testified to in the Holy Scriptures. The theological structure of Lutheranism is Christological; every theological theme is explicated from the summit of revelation which is Christ. The doctrines of God, Man, Sin, Church, the Sacraments, are inwardly formed and illumined by the light received in Christ. Of God, the fundamental assertion is that He is the Creator who in the Christ-event restores to filial relationship and purpose his lost children. Man, it is asserted, knows who he is only in the light of God's revelation to him and action for him in Christ. He is thus revealed as sinner, that is, in separation from God. This alienation is a thoroughly religious fact in Lutheran understanding, and its reality, evident, to be sure, in man's psychic, moral, and historical career, is never to be identified with such evidence. Sin, that is to say, is coterminous with man's being and is not to be isolated or adequately contained in categories of psychology, ethics, or sociology. Sin is fundamentally a radical egocentricity by virtue of which man seeks himself in everything.

The Incarnation of God in Christ is therefore revelatory of the corruption of man's relationship with God along the entire front of his being, and declarative of the purpose, power, and ingressive love of God.

The church is the communion of all those who hear the call of the action of God in Christ; its marks are the declaration of the gospel and the response of love and obedience in the celebration of the two sacraments of the gospel, Baptism and the Lord's Supper. The church is described in the Augsburg Confession as the Communion of Saints in which the gospel is rightly preached (and heard) and the sacraments rightly administered. In Luther's explanation of the third article of the Creed is a compressed statement of what Lutherans believe concerning spirit, church, and faith:

The Holy Ghost has called me through the Gospel, enlightened me with His Gifts, and sanctified and preserved me in the true faith; in like manner as He calls, gathers, enlightens, and sanctifies the whole Christian church, and preserves it in union with Jesus Christ in the one true faith.

Here it is asserted that the gospel is inert save for the vivifying activity of God's Spirit. Just as the redemption of the individual is to be ascribed to the gracious activity of the Holy Spirit, so, too, the existence and reality of the church is a creation of the same spirit.

Lutheran understanding of the Scriptures prevents every effort to handle them in such a way as to derive a legal or historically absolute order for the church therefrom. The doctrines of church and ministry are rather derived from the gospel of God's redemption in Christ. This gospel declares God's purpose to create a redeemed community, the church, and it is the function of the Spirit in that community to exercise through it the endless vitality of the call of God in Christ. Ministry is a common responsibility of the faithful, and imposes upon all the priesthood of their faith. Lutherans recognize, to be sure, a specific ministry of the Word and Sacrament, and the church ordains to this ministry those who receive a vocation and honor it by the discipline of theological studies.

The church is ordered from above by the gospel. Any order which is serviceable to the proclamation of the gospel and the preservation of the sacraments is a legitimate order. It is not held necessary that human ordinances, organization, and rites be everywhere the same.

Inasmuch as Lutheranism acknowledges its unity in common confessions, and not in common orders, varying forms of organization in its order cannot be adequately described in a generalization. During and after the spread of the Reformation movement in many European lands in the sixteenth century, congregations which found the Lutheran confessions expressive of their renewed understanding of the gospel were established in the context of many and various political and social situations. The churches in these situations adapted their order to the existing circumstances, and these varieties of relationship to public order remain to this day. The *Landeskirschen* in Germany, the quasi-establishment in the Scandinavian countries, and the congregational polity in the Americas are illustrations of this variety.

It is only against this extremely variegated and complicated European background that the plurality of Lutheran Church bodies in America can be understood. The Reformation was followed by large-scale emigration to America; and over a period of more than three hundred years, this emigration brought Lutheran people to America from virtually every Continental nation. They brought with them their Bibles, prayer books and hymnals, confessional writings and devotional manuals, in the language of their homeland. And inasmuch as the Lutherans were among the first to penetrate and settle along the expanding North American and Canadian frontier, the resultant linguistic barrier, both as among Lutherans from various lands and between many Lutherans and their fellow Christians on this continent, has persisted to our time. Only within the twentieth century indeed have several of the largest bodies of Lutherans in America become English-speaking churches.

The present baptized membership of the Lutheran churches in the United States and Canada is about four and a half million souls. The largest concentrations are in the seaboard states, throughout the Middle West, and in the states of the nearer Northwest. The earlier settlements are reflective of the coming of European peoples to America in colonial times; the later settlements reflect the huge nineteenth century wave of emigration from Germany and the Scandinavian countries.

WALTER G. MUELDER

⋖⋗

Methodism

Methodism's theological perspectives are best understood in relation to what some of its leaders have considered to be the cardinal principles of protestantism, and especially of the evangelical revival of the eighteenth century. The power of the Wesleyan movement was in part due to the timeliness of its message. Certain emphases in its theology reflect the needs of that age and the spirit of both intellectual and practical relevance in succeeding centuries.

Among the cardinal principles of protestantism which Methodists stress are: (1) the authority of Scripture; (2) the right of private judgment, with its implications for the idea of tolerance and religious liberty; (3) justification by faith; (4) freedom of will (breaking sharply here with predestination); (5) the sanctity of the common life; and (6) faith as both a human and a divine act, stressing moral and rational elements in faith, the divine initiative through grace, and the importance of religious experience.

The preaching of John Wesley was an Arminianism that announced salvation as available to all men and not simply to an elect few. Christ died for all men, and any man is free to

accept this salvation. All could become actual sons of God. To
the gospel of God's grace was added the idea of conscious salvation. Those whose sins God forgives, he assures by an inner
voice that they are his children. God's grace is constantly available to men and endows them daily with strength for the work
of life. There is thus a great stress on the work of the Holy
Spirit. Along with a doctrine of justification by faith, Wesley
laid on his converts the responsibilities of love. The new life in
Christ could be made perfect in love, sanctification as well as
justification being embraced in salvation. Forgiveness and
sanctification are the two cardinal factors in the idea of salvation. Forgiveness, based on atonement, is the ground of the
Christian life; yet sanctification dominates Wesley's thought
because salvation is seen as a process directed to the perfect,
real change of the individual. As justified by faith, man is accepted by God as one of His children; but this experienced
judgment of grace stands in tension with the coming judgment
of works, the final salvation for which the maturing power of
sanctification will qualify him.

Methodism owes much to the Church of England. Not least
is the fact that her Articles of Religion are the Thirty-nine
Articles of the Church of England reduced to twenty-five. The
Articles of Religion, however, are not a confining theological
fence. They provide a significant historical point of reference;
but they are also a starting point of theological exploration.
Taken by themselves, they do not fully express the experi-
mental spirit of Methodism as an individual and social force.

One of the summaries of distinctive Methodist emphasis
which Wesley formulated says:

What was their fundamental doctrine? That the Bible is
the whole and sole rule both of Christian faith and practice.

Hence they learned, (1) That religion is an inward principle; that it is no other than the mind that was in Christ; or,
in other words, the renewal of the soul after the image of
God, in righteousness and true holiness. (2) That this can
never be wrought in us, but by the power of the Holy Ghost.
(3) That we receive this, and every other blessing, merely
for the sake of Christ: and (4) That whosoever hath the
mind that was in Christ, the same is our brother, and sister,
and mother.

In 1777, John and Charles Wesley prepared a hymnal intended for "the Use of Christians of all Denominations." Its
preface sounds a significant ecumenical note:

> The ease and happiness that attend, the unspeakable ad-
> vantages that flow from, a truly catholic spirit, a spirit of
> universal love (which is the very reverse of bigotry), one
> would imagine, might recommend this amiable temper to
> every person of cool reflection. And who that has tasted of
> this happiness can refrain from wishing it to all mankind?
> . . . It is with unspeakable joy, that these observe the spirit
> of bigotry greatly declining (at least, in every Protestant
> nation of Europe), and the spirit of love proportionably in-
> creasing. Men of every opinion and denomination now begin
> to bear with each other. They seem weary of tearing each
> other to pieces on account of small and unessential differ-
> ences; and rather desire to build up each other in the great
> point wherein they all agree—the faith which worketh by
> love, and produces in them the mind which was in Jesus
> Christ. It is hoped, the ensuing collection of Hymns may in
> some measure contribute, through the blessing of God, to
> advance this glorious end, to promote this spirit of love, not
> confined to any opinion or party. There is not a hynm, not

one verse, inserted here, but what relates to the common salvation; and what every serious and unprejudiced Christian, of whatever denomination, may join in.

The Wesleys may have been in error in some details of theological selection in the verses and hymns, but the spirit which animated their evangelical fervor has left a deep imprint on Methodist readiness for ecumenical experience.

In addition to doctrinal dependence, we may note other significant factors of indebtedness to the Church of England which help in understanding the order and organization of Methodism. There is, first of all, a rich churchly heritage and tradition which assisted Methodism from being confined as a merely sect institution. The fervor of evangelical Christianity was fed by the many-sidedness of the great Anglican tradition. Secondly, Methodism inherited a dignified worship and historic liturgy. The rituals of baptism, marriage, ordination, burial ceremonies, and the sacrament of the Lord's Supper owe much to the Prayer Book of the Church of England. So also is the tradition of an official and dignified hymnody. Thirdly, the form of church government is based on the Low Church Anglican concepts of church polity. Wesley held with Luther that there is no form of church government prescribed in Scripture, but held that the episcopal form was not contrary to Scripture. The conception of ministerial orders and the nature of their functions are Anglican. Methodism approved, adopted, and used the forms and methods of a historic ministry. These it adapted to the social and historical circumstances of the people whom it served. Thus, for example, the episcopacy has never in Methodism been considered a "third order," but rather the investiture of an "elder" with certain definite executive functions and powers. As a consequence, the Methodist bishops "not only have no power to ordain a person for the episcopal office till he be first elected by the General Conference, but they possess no authority to ordain an elder or a traveling deacon till he be first elected by a yearly Conference."

The functioning organization of the Methodist Church comprises a General Conference for the entire church, Jurisdictional Conferences for the church in the U.S.A., Central Conferences for the church outside the United States of America, and Annual Conferences as the fundamental bodies in the church. The General Conference meets quadrennially and is composed of not less than six hundred or more than eight hundred delegates, equally divided among ministers and laymen (including laywomen), all elected by Annual Conferences. The General Conference has full legislative power over all matters distinctively connectional. The bishops are elected in Jurisdictional Conferences, which otherwise are functional auxiliary bodies to promote the general interests of the church. The Annual Conference—composed of both ministers and laymen—is the basic body in the church. As such, it has reserved the right to vote on all constitutional amendments, on the election of all delegates to General, Jurisdictional, and Central Conferences, on all matters relating to ministerial relations and ordination, except that lay members may not vote on matters of ordination, character, and Conference relations of ministers. In addition to the Conferences, there are the episcopacy and the Judiciary. A council of bishops provides administrative leadership and presidential supervision for the jurisdictions and areas. The Judiciary functions as a supreme ecclesiastical court on specified matters of church law.

There are about nine million members of the Methodist Church in the U.S.A., served through about forty thousand preaching places. In all, there are twenty-three bodies in the country bearing the Methodist name. Most of these represent schisms or withdrawals from other Methodist bodies. In addition, there are about a dozen groups which may be termed quasi-Methodist sects. They profess to be Wesleyan in doctrine, they were organized by Methodists and drew their original members mainly from the Methodist constituency. About two dozen other sects espouse the sanctification doctrine promulgated by early Methodist preachers. The fifty or more sects traceable to Methodism have a combined membership of nearly ten million persons. The Methodist Church is widely distributed over the nation, with special strength in the middle western and southern states.

PAUL LEHMANN

❦

The Presbyterian Churches

Presbyterian churches in the United States belong to the general type or family of churches known as "Reformed." During the Reformation in the sixteenth century, a difference of emphasis in matters of doctrine and a difference in the form of church government rather quickly emerged between the churches in the orbit of Luther's influence and the churches under the influence of Calvin. The Calvinistic churches were called "Reformed" to distinguish them from the churches called "Lutheran." These two types of churches also came to be distinguishable geographically. Broadly speaking, the Lutherans settled down in Germany and Scandinavia; the Reformed in Switzerland, the Netherlands, France, and Scotland.

In the United States, the Reformed churches are more commonly known by other names. Some groups have kept the term "Reformed" and have added to it a qualifying word or phrase, such as the Christian Reformed Church, the Evangelical and Reformed Church, the Reformed Church in America. But by far the largest number of churches in the United States which are descended from the Reformed or Calvinistic branch of the

Reformation are called "Presbyterian." They are called Presbyterian because of the form of government which obtains among them. The life and work of these churches is chiefly ordered through presbyteries, that is, delegated assemblies of presbyters, or elders. Numerically considered, the three largest Presbyterian churches in the United States are known (in ascending order) as the United Presbyterian Church; the Presbyterian Church in the United States; and the Presbyterian Church in the United States of America. (The latter two of these bodies owe their separate existence to the American Civil War.) According to its statistical record for the year 1951, the Presbyterian Church in the United States of America has a membership of 2,447,975. The greatest concentration of members, ministers, and churches is in the eastern part of the United States (Pennsylvania, New York, and New Jersey), although Illinois and California are also notable centers of this Presbyterian group. It is perhaps worth noting in this connection that active conversations are going on, looking toward a union of the United Presbyterian Church, the Presbyterian Church in the United States, and the Presbyterian Church in the United States of America. Because it is clearer to deal with a single church, we shall here speak of the Presbyterian Church in the U.S.A., in the recognition that the others are similar.

Any person may become a member of the Presbyterian Church U.S.A. (as it is usually called) who, being baptized, reaffirms his Christian faith. It is important to note that no particular creedal formulation is required. The order for Baptism for adults not previously baptized asks the believer to declare his faith in God the Father Almighty, in Jesus Christ His only Son, and in the Holy Spirit. There is a further acknowledgment of the need for the forgiveness of sins, of trust

in God's mercy in Jesus Christ, and of willingness to partici-
pate in the worship and the fellowship of the church.

Ministers and elders of the Presbyterian Church are, however, committed to more specifically formulated obligations.
These include the acknowledgment of the Scripture of the Old
and New Testaments to be the Word of God, "the only infalli-
ble rule of faith and practice"; the acceptance of the Westminster Confession of Faith as "containing the system of doctrine taught in the Holy Scriptures"; and the approval of "the
government and discipline of the Presbyterian Church in the
United States of America." The Constitution of the Church is a
composite document of faith and order. It consists of the Westminster Confession of Faith; the Larger and Shorter Catechisms; the Form of Government; the Book of Discipline; and
the Directory for the Worship of God. With the exception of
the Catechisms, the various parts of the Constitution have been
frequently amended since their adoption in the eighteenth century.

It is evident from this conspicuous difference between the
commitments asked of members and the commitments asked of
ministers and elders that the Presbyterian Church has a "high
doctrine" of the ministry and of church order. A high doctrine
of the ministry is one which regards the ministry in some way
as belonging to the essential nature of the church. The Presbyterian Church stands between the sacramental-hierarchical
view of the ministry in Catholicism (Roman, Eastern Orthodox,
and Anglo-Catholic) and the congregational-functional view of
the ministry in Congregationalism and the so-called "free
churches." The grounds for this position are chiefly two: scriptural and theological. The scriptural ground points to the
dominant role of the Apostles in the life of the New Testament
churches. The Presbyterian Church believes in an apostolic

ministry, but does not regard the manner of succession as definitive. The marks of the apostolate are derived from the commission of Jesus to preach and to teach, and from faithfulness to the "Word of God" revealed in the Bible. The theological ground for the Presbyterian view of the ministry is derived from John Calvin's insistence upon the fact that God works instrumentally and from the importance which Calvin attached to the "right" preaching of the Word and administration of the sacraments in the church.

The Presbyterian Church undertakes to guard against excessive ministerial authority by a division of powers and functions in a representative form of government. The governmental structure is composed of a series of policy-making bodies, beginning with the session, or council of teaching and ruling elders of the local congregation, and extending through presbyteries and synods to the General Assembly, the highest judicatory of the church. Each of these judicatories possesses executive, legislative, and judicial powers. It is significant, especially from an ecumenical standpoint, that while the Presbyterian Church declares that "it is absolutely necessary that the government of the Church be exercised under some certain and definite form," it also asserts that "we embrace in the spirit of charity, those Christians who differ from us, in opinion, or in practice, on these subjects." The Presbyterian Church expresses this "spirit of charity" at least in its practice of ordination. Ministers are ordained not only to the Presbyterian Church but as ministers in the church universal. Although women may be ordained as elders, ordination to the ministry is reserved to men.

The distinctive feature of the Presbyterian Church U.S.A. (and of other Presbyterian bodies as well) is the presbyterial and representative governmental structure. It is not easy to be as definite about theological doctrine. The Presbyterian Church is not alone in accepting the central importance of the Bible as the primary source of Christian knowledge and instruction. In common with many other churches, the Presbyterian Church holds to the trinitarian understanding of God's nature and activity as this understanding is expressed in such confessions of faith as the Apostles' and the Nicene Creeds. Indeed, the rubric for ordination to the ministry affirms the trinitarian faith of "the Holy Catholic or Universal Church" as the basis on which the vows are taken. Beyond these, however, the Presbyterian Church assigns a place of special eminence in matters of doctrine to the Westminster Confession of Faith. This document is said to contain "the system of doctrine taught in the Holy Scriptures." In practice, the Westminster Confession has often been regarded with an authority which made its statements binding both in content and in form. But this uncritical literalism is contradicted by the Confession itself. The Confession declares that "synods and councils . . . are not to be made the rule of faith or practice, but to be used as a help in both" (Chapter 31). It further declares the Holy Scripture "to be the rule of faith and life" (Chapter 1).

When the Confession is read in the light of Scripture, the following doctrines may be mentioned as expressing the main theological emphases of the Presbyterian Church, U.S.A.:

1. *The Authority of the Bible, as the Word of God*

God has made himself known in a personal way to persons, uniquely in Jesus Christ, and through the words of the authors of the biblical writings, whose words help us to understand the unique significance of Jesus Christ. The authority of the Bible has often been held to be proved from its inerrant statements.

The Confession, however, makes it plain that the authority of the Bible depends "wholly upon God" and requires "the inward illumination of the Spirit of God" rightly to be understood.

2. *The Sovereignty of God*

God is to be honored and obeyed above all else in the world, since the world and all things in it depend for their existence upon God's power and will, and since the world and all things in it have meaning and purpose in the light of the purposes of God.

3. *The Divine Election*

This doctrine is often confused with predeterminism, as though God had determined in advance everything that man could do, or that was going to happen to man, thus nullifying man's own activity and decisions. Election means exactly the contrary. It refers to the question of whether man's actions and decisions have any meaning in the light of circumstances and a future over which man has no control. The doctrine of election asserts that a man's future is a matter of destiny and that the fulfillment of human destiny is neither accidental nor the result of man's efforts. It is guaranteed instead by the sovereign will and purpose of God.

4. *The Divine Providence*

The idea is that God has not merely started the world but works continually in it to achieve his purposes. Whereas elec-

tion has to do with the destiny of man, providence has to do
with the stability and order of the world.

5. *The Total Depravity of Man*

The idea is not that man can do no good, but that man cannot either of his own volition or his own ability achieve salvation, that is, the fulfillment of his life in accordance with
God's purposes.

6. *The Lordship of Christ*

The idea is that Jesus of Nazareth, as the revealer of God
and the saviour of men and the world, continues to be actively
at work in the world, commanding the loyalty and obedience
of men and bringing God's purposes to fruition by overcoming
all human resistance.

7. *The Catholic or Universal Church*

The idea is that the revealing and saving activity of Jesus
Christ has a specific place and focus in the world. This place
and focus is the church, the Body, of which Christ is the Head.
Of the ministry and the government of the church mention has
already been made. Here it will be sufficient to note the stress
upon the visible and world-wide character of the fellowship of
believers, as the instrument and evidence of the saving activity
of Jesus Christ in the world.

POWEL MILLS DAWLEY

≈§₺≈

The Protestant Episcopal Church

The Protestant Episcopal Church in the United States of America is one of the dozen independent national churches and ecclesiastical provinces, all linked historically with the Church of England, which together comprise the family of churches known as the Anglican Communion. Originally formed by the overseas expansion of the English Church in the wake of England's spreading imperial power, these churches rapidly spread beyond the bounds of English-speaking peoples. The missionary enterprise of the nineteenth century carried them throughout the world. Today, in America, Africa, and Asia, churches once bearing marks of their English origin have become truly indigenous in character.

Remarkably enough, no authoritative canonical framework or central ecclesiastical jurisdiction holds these independent churches together. Their unity is deeper than that. It is based upon the heritage of a common faith, the experience of a common liturgy, and the adherence to a common episcopal church order. For Anglicans throughout the world, these elements in their church life are not only the true ground of catholic unity but also the guarantees of continuity with the church's life through all the ages. History has decisive claims upon Anglicans; continuity was of primary importance in their Reformation experience.

Within this unity and communion, complete regional autonomy is possessed by the separate members of the Anglican Fellowship of Churches. For example, each church has its own body of Constitutions and Canons. While each church has maintained the historic episcopal ministry at the center of its order, local adaptation in the area of constitutional church government is considerable. The *Book of Common Prayer*, accepted everywhere as the general Anglican standard of doctrine and practice, has undergone frequent revision, largely in the direction of flexibility and enrichment, in the different autonomous churches. The central consultative body in the Anglican Communion is the Lambeth Conference, a meeting at stated intervals of all bishops of the whole communion, under the presidence of the Archbishop of Canterbury. While decisions and resolutions of the Conference command no canonical obedience and are not binding upon the separate churches, they carry great moral authority throughout the whole Fellowship.

Within this communion the Protestant Episcopal Church finds its continuity with the historic Catholic Church. The history of the formation of the Protestant Episcopal Church illustrates the capacity of Anglicanism to adapt itself to new conditions and circumstances, and yet maintain the continuity of its own tradition. Before the American Revolution, Anglican parishes existed, under the supervision of the Bishop of London, in all the Atlantic colonies, formed there by the English settlers in the early seventeenth century. Their strength and influence in the colonial religious scene varied from a somewhat precarious hold in Puritan New England to a legal establishment in Virginia and other royalist colonies. The American Revolution, separating the colonies from the English crown, severed the Anglican parishes from the English Church as far as their government was concerned. At once the American congregations launched themselves upon the bold experiment of the formation of an independent church of the Anglican Communion outside the British Isles. Here the local initiative and sense of responsibility that had developed under the peculiar American conditions displayed its vigor. Within a few years the scattered parishes were formed into dioceses and united in a national organization, an episcopate was secured from the Church of England and the Scottish Episcopal Church, and an American Prayer Book and Constitution adopted.

Constitutionally, the Episcopal Church revived the ancient principle of church government through representative synods, with the significant admission of laymen to a direct voice and vote in the affairs of the church. The basic administrative unit is the diocese. There the bishop, shedding the ancient prelatical powers of sole ruler, shares the responsibilities of leadership and government with both clergy and laymen. The hundred or so dioceses of the Episcopal Church are represented in a triennial General Convention, the bicameral legislative body of the national organization. Decisions are reached by joint action of a House of Bishops and a House of Clerical and Lay Deputies. The task of continuing administration is entrusted by General Convention to a National Council which, in its permanent departments of domestic and foreign missions, Christian education, social relations, finance, and so forth, carries on the ordinary work of the national church. The chief executive officer is the Presiding Bishop, at once the president of the Council and the House of Bishops.

Today the concentration of communicant strength of the

Episcopal Church still reflects its long association with the colonies and states of the Atlantic seaboard. The total number of baptized Episcopalians is slightly over two and a half millions, with approximately half of these located in New England, New York, the Middle States, and Virginia. But with the largest proportional gains in recent years in the far western dioceses, this concentration is slowly disappearing. Within the whole country, the strength of the Episcopal Church is chiefly urban. The relatively small number of dioceses that contain the largest American cities also contain over two-fifths of the members of the church. Yet here, too, recent statistics show a gradual change. The greatest percentage gains are now consistently in the rural dioceses.

With the other churches of the Anglican Communion the Episcopal Church shares a common faith, order, and experience of worship. Its faith is enshrined in the historic catholic creeds of Christendom, the affirmations of the central dogmas of Christianity in which the redemptive acts of God in history are set forth. At the time of the Reformation, the Church of England formulated no comprehensive and authoritative Confession of the type that distinguished the doctrinal formularies of Continental protestantism. Instead, the Anglican appeal was to Holy Scripture and to its interpretation by the ancient Fathers of the undivided church, to the Ecumenical Councils, and to the free *consensus fidelium*—that is, the continuing experience of the Holy Spirit through His faithful people in the church.

The flexibility of this principle of authority made possible the peculiar mark of the Anglican Reformation experience— first, continuity in the life of the church with catholic faith and order, now freed from the authoritarian rigidity and narrow dogmatism of papalism; secondly, comprehension in the unity of one Fellowship of those who emphasized different approaches to truth. Tension became inevitable in such a communion, and is still part of the Anglican ethos. But the Anglican maintains this tension to be creative. It makes possible a deeper understanding of the wholeness of God's truth in His Church. At best, truth is seen to lie in the conjunction of the things Christians call "catholic" and "evangelical."

The common experience of worship in the churches of the Anglican Communion is secured by their heritage of a common liturgy. Whatever may be the variations among the Prayer Books of the different autonomous churches, they are slight compared with the liturgical patterns of prayer and sacrament common to all. The *Book of Common Prayer* is at once a standard of doctrine and practice for Episcopalians, and at the same time the means of uniting them with corporate spiritual experiences of prayer, adoration, praise, and sacrament of the church through the ages.

The bond of a common church order among Anglican churches is seen in their perpetuation of an episcopate maintained in unbroken apostolic succession. In Anglican thought, the ministry is regarded as an original and essential element in the Christian Fellowship, the organ of both its continuity and unity. Fundamentally, there is no impassable gulf between the church or its lay members and the ordained ministry. The latter represents and functions for the whole Body in those responsibilities of priestly vocation in which all the members of the church are by nature involved. The ordained ministers perform those special functions necessary both for the continuance of the church's life and the fulfillment of the task of the whole Body of Christ.

The ordained Anglican ministry is the ancient catholic ministry of threefold order: bishops, priests, and deacons. Each has a distinct sacramental character, conferred in episcopal ordination; each has separate liturgical and pastoral functions. The historic episcopate is the source and center of this ministry, the bishop not only forming the historic link with the apostolic mission and authority but also representing the principle of Fatherhood in the household of God. In his official capacity the bishop brings the unity and authority of the whole church into his diocese, and similarly, his diocese into the greater church.

The elements of faith and order that any communion holds to be essential are often best summarized in its attempts to formulate a basis upon which negotiations for Christian reunion may take place. In 1888, the Lambeth Conference set forth the famous Quadrilateral, essentials upon which any unity must rest: (1) the Holy Scriptures of the Old and New Testaments, as containing all things necessary to salvation, and as being the rule and ultimate standard of faith; (2) the Apostles' Creed as the Baptismal Symbol, and the Nicene Creed as the sufficient statement of the Christian Faith; (3) the two sacraments ordained by Christ himself—Baptism and the Supper of the Lord—ministered with unfailing use of Christ's words of Institution, and of the elements ordained by him; (4) the Historic Episcopate, locally adapted in the methods of its administration to the varying needs of the nations and peoples called of God into the unity of His Church.

ERROL T. ELLIOTT

&⚬⚬⚬&

Society of Friends

The Society of Friends, commonly known as Quakers, has never, since its rise three hundred years ago (about 1652) in the Northwest of England, had a common and formal doctrinal statement. Indeed, in its first decades, the Society was contraposed to the creedal and ritualistic practices of the churches of that day by the very principles on which it took its rise.

Breaking from the restraints on the free spirit which Friends felt the churches imposed, they went quite to the opposite position, placing their reliance upon an immediate (unmediated), personal and individual experience of God within. They were so released from the "letter" to the "spirit" that they generally even looked with disfavor on the reading of the Scriptures in their public Meetings for Worship.

Despite this attitude, there is every evidence that they held in general what are now considered orthodox points of view, and in that light believed in the Bible and the use of it. They thought and lived definitely within the Christian tradition. In the spirit of George Fox, founder of the Quakers, they raised the question continually as to whether professing believers had

177

"come into that spirit of life and power in which they were who gave forth the Scriptures." Their emphasis was on the spirit back of the words, yet they often quoted from the Scriptures and based their faith on its message, as they understood it.

The Gospel according to John was especially basic to their faith, with their emphasis on the inner light or "that of God in everyman." This spiritual inheritance of the race, this light within, was not an end in itself, not their salvation, but their means to salvation. It is now often called "the light of Christ." This faith placed an emphasis in their life and ministry—a high expectancy from men, a great potential for human redemption, and a sensitiveness to the needs of men in their relation with one another. Their best-known witness is their opposition to war.

It might be said that *instead of creeds* the Quakers developed unwritten "testimonies," such as testimonies on peace and on simplicity "in dress and address," that is, in apparel and in speech. Integrity was the hallmark of their common witness. Hence, the formal oath required of them in their day was the chief reason for their numerous imprisonments for the public practice of their emancipating faith. As they were brought into court, they insisted that their simple affirmation of "yea and nay" could not be strengthened, indeed would be weakened, by profuse and formal "swearing," and they quoted Scripture against it. Theirs was a distinction between the spirit of integrity and the elaboration of words, whether the issue was in taking the formal oath or in subscribing to creeds, which were "other men's words."

The body of literature relating to the faith of these early Friends consists chiefly of travel journals and letters which conveyed their beliefs and interpretations. These have formed the basis for compilations of their writings and for many statements variously called "Discipline," "Faith and Practice," and other titles under which Friends have, in more recent years, tried to indicate their faith, witness, and business procedures. For reasons that are stated in the following paragraphs, none of these statements has been endorsed nor can be officially approved by the Religious Society of Friends as a whole.

The Yearly Meetings of Friends (similar to Annual Conferences), of which there are fifty-three in the world, present diversity in their statements, both on faith and on business practices. Few of the Yearly Meetings have identical statements. Some of their "Disciplines" represent an evangelical, orthodox emphasis, and are accepted by some Friends as wellnigh having the force of a creed. Other statements are broad and liberal in spirit, and are accepted as advices rather than as a definitive statement of faith. There seems to be at present a growing interest among Friends in developing a clearer concept of faith and order, within the general pattern of the Christian tradition. The ecumenical movement has stimulated their interest in finding the contribution which Friends should make in the Christian church, and among the churches.

The loosely knit order which the Quaker movement developed was the logical outcome of their attitude, indicated above. The avoidance of all ecclesiasticism and central authority produced an order largely individualistic, yet disciplined by group thought. Instead of one person being given authority, it was the Meeting (now spelled with a capital) which checked the "leadings" of the individual member—restraining, encouraging, or counseling him. Overseers, and especially elders, were appointed to have particular concern for the spiritual and moral welfare of the members.

These Meetings (like local churches) came to be organized

as Monthly Meetings for Business to care for the physical and spiritual aspects of the membership. Later, Monthly Meetings were grouped as Quarterly Meetings, and these in turn constituted Yearly Meetings within limited geographical areas.

In America some of these Yearly Meetings now constitute the Friends General Conference, generally liberal in persuasion, while certain others compose the Five Years Meeting of Friends, more evangelical in policy. There are yet other independent Yearly Meetings, some of which tend toward conservatism in Quaker traditions or in doctrines, or both, while others are more liberal.

During the American migrations of the nineteenth century, and under the influence of the great evangelical movement, a "pastoral system" came into existence to meet the needs of Quaker communities isolated from other Meetings, primarily from those in more densely populated areas on the Atlantic Coast which retained the traditional Quaker practices. Today about one-half of the Friends of the world are affiliated with each pattern of life and procedure—those of the traditional open Meeting and those of the pastoral, more evangelical persuasion.

There are about one hundred and sixteen thousand Quakers in the United States, with their greatest concentrations of population in Pennsylvania and Indiana. From the period of the great migrations which helped to produce their diversities, they are now returning to a revived fellowship through world, national, and regional conferences, and through the American Friends Service Committee, which has furnished the chief connecting links since its formation in 1917. The Friends Fellowship Council (an American organization), the Friends World Committee for Consultation (a world-wide fellowship), and the Friends Committee on National Legislation are three other general bodies whose functions bring Friends generally into a closer relationship. None of these, however, is prepared to speak or act officially for the Society of Friends as a whole. The Yearly Meetings are autonomous bodies, though in the case of the Five Years Meetings certain responsibilities are vested in the larger body.

Taken as a whole, the Quaker order of life was from the beginning, and is yet, more a Christian movement than a sect.